The Fundamentals of Data Science

Big Data, Deep Learning, and Machine Learning: What you need to know about data science and why it matters

Author: Vlad Sozonov

Table of Contents

Book Description: Fundamentals of Data Science

Data science is no easy term to define. While there are many definitions available that point out its statistical or logical aspects, others focus on its machine learning impacts. The truth is, data science is a process that requires an understanding of multiple fields, methods, techniques, and more. Data science cannot be easily labeled because, when applied, it looks different to each person, business, or organization utilizing it. While the term may not be easy to define, what it is used for, can be used for, and approaches to it can be more easily understood. And that is precisely what this book aims to do.

This book will not only thoroughly go over all the skills, people, and steps involved in data science, it will also look closely at:

- What big data is and how data science came from it.
- How data has evolved, resulting in new methods for understanding it.
- How data science influenced artificial intelligence.
- How data science is used in machine learning and deep learning.
- How data science revolutionizes the way we train machines and set up neural networks.

Data science, big data, machine learning, and deep learning tend to intimidate people. Many believe it is too complicated or technology-centered for them to break into these fields. This book is designed to simplify these complex areas in a way that anyone can understand the fundamentals. Whether you are just hearing about data science, are a student studying it in college, or looking to expand your career, this book has something to offer every type of data enthusiast.

Introduction

Today, our world is primarily data-driven. Data is everywhere and can be obtained through any and every action you take, especially on mobile devices or through the use of the Internet. Data holds the key to future possibilities. It has already changed and shaped so many areas of our daily lives and the way businesses operate.

Groundbreaking technologies have swept through industries, opening opportunities for further exploration in the way data can be used. From automation systems to predictive tools, data is at the core of just about every business move. It is also what makes many of our daily burdens, chores, and to-dos much more convenient. For instance, how would you have been able to calculate the time needed to travel from work to your child's soccer game to ensure you made it on time 20 years ago? How could you have known about the ratings of the new restaurant down the street if you couldn't just pull out your phone to check? What about self-driving cars, or recommendations for movies to watch on Netflix? All this is possible because of data.

It is hard to imagine just how much data is available today. So much so that a new way of funneling through, organizing, and making use of this data has brought about the evolution of a whole new science. Data science is a by-product of the massive amounts of data that drives so much of the world. It isn't a completely new way of handling data, but it is a highly innovative and ever-changing way regarding how we approach data.

For businesses, this new wave of data from endless sources, with the help of data science, equates to unlimited opportunities to improve and change the way they operate. Industries have seen phenomenal shifts in efficiency, reliability, and success from uncovering insightful information from collected data. For many, it is hard to make sense of just how data can have such an impact, and that is precisely what data science does.

Data science is a term that encompasses a variety of smaller parts. While it may seem quite complex, when it is broken down to its core components, it is much easier to comprehend. Throughout this book, you will not only gain an in-depth understanding of what data science is, but we will examine specific areas where data science plays a significant role.

Data science fits into a number of technology-driven fields, such as artificial intelligence. It is used to understand what predictions machine-learning models should be taught. Data science is used to spot trends and patterns that machine-learning models will be able to mimic or process in real-time to enhance customer satisfaction. This machine learning is how your email is able to filter out spam, or your e-reader shows a convenient list of book recommendations based on your most recent reads. It is also how medical diagnoses are able to be made in less time and how symptoms can be treated before they become life-threatening. From data comes knowledge, and from that knowledge, there have been born new ways of doing things that have improved the quality of life and life expectancy of many.

This book will not only highlight how data science is used in these unimaginable ways, but will also explain how it is used with advanced technologies like machine learning, deep learning, and neural networks. From the start of a data science project to the final presentation, you will have a clear grasp of all things data science that will lay the foundation for learning so much more.

Chapter 1
Introduction to Data Science

"The goal is to turn data into information and information into insight."

-Carly Fiorina

What is Data Science?

Data science is derived from data mining. Data mining refers to the ability to find patterns in data, which uses database theories and statistical methodology to analyze, store, and gain insight from massive amounts of data. Database theories focus on understanding complex languages and logic used among databases and database management systems. Statistical methodologies are the formulas, techniques, and models used to perform statistical analysis of raw data. Data mining was a popular way to gain a deeper appreciation of data obtained by businesses, but as the technology has improved, data has grown substantially—to the point where data mining alone cannot possibly filter through the quantity of available raw data.

Data science is an expansion of data mining. In simplest terms, data science involves using data to gain a better understanding of trends or patterns to make more sound decisions. Data science examines an abundant amount of data and therefore, can uncover many more previously unknown facts. But data science is much more complicated than just gathering information. It utilizes a combination of algorithms, tools, principles, the scientific method, and additional analytics to make use of large quantities of data from various sources. The primary goal of data science is to obtain valuable information from collected data, and then communicate the value and present it in visual form.

Data science has been gaining the attention of businesses across the globe, both large and small. It is used to keep track of customers, sales, productivity, efficiency, across all industries to not just grow as a business, but to improve the way business is done. This is why data science and business intelligence are often misused and confused. Both use data to help make informed decisions, but the kind of data used and the deciphering of this data look astonishingly different.

The difference between data science and business intelligence, or BI, comes down to how the data is used with both. With business intelligence, the data is measured and then presented. It focuses primarily on past and present data. Data science goes beyond this to explain why the collected data was used, how it was used and dives into how to use this data to control outcomes and make justified predictions for the future. Those working on a data science project should, however, have a clear understanding of business intelligence. This is an often-overlooked aspect of data science that can greatly benefit your project.

Clearly understanding the business you are working with to solve a specific problem is essential in data science. When you have a certain amount of business intelligence, you are able to ask the right questions. These questions are what will drive where and how you gather your data.

What does Data Science Involve?

There is a lot more to data science than simply making sense of data. A number of skills are required in order to accurately transform data into useful information. While all of the following data science elements are not necessary for every project, one should have a clear understanding of what each of the following is, how to perform each one, and when each is best used for optimal results.

Database Management

The data used in data science needs to be properly stored in one place for each project or future use. You need to be able to easily store, retrieve, update, and read data on a regular basis. The right database management system is vital to make this process as seamless as possible. Relational database management systems such as SQL are one of the first systems that come to mind when data is involved. An SQL allows you to customize the database to make it easier to gain more knowledge from your specific datasets. These are one of the simplest systems to learn and are highly effective at indexing the variables of data in clearly defined tables and columns. But SQL is not the only type of database management system you will want to have an understanding of.

NoSQL databases are better equipped to handle big data. These can be used for various data models and can accommodate higher volumes of information. NoSQL databases are more flexible than relational database management systems, and updates to indexes are less time-consuming. Understanding the database management systems available and which ones are best suited for which types of data is essential in data science.

Data Acquisition

Data science requires obtaining data and establishing datasets from a number of sources. Data acquisition refers to the ability to gather data and configure it into useful information. This can be in the form of configuring APIs, exploring databases, or searching the Internet for reliable data that can be used for processing. While data acquisition is being performed, it is also vital that data is checked to ensure the latest information is being used, and the location it is retrieved from is tracked.

Data Entry

You will need to know how to properly enter data into a computer system or an online database. You should have an understanding of the tools available to assist in data entry. Having a fast and accurate typing speed will make this area of data science less cumbersome.

Data Extraction

Data extraction is the process of replacing values in a data set that are missing or that may be read as having non-values. This can be a time-consuming process where all the data is carefully reviewed in order to process the information efficiently. Since most data obtained in data science tends to be unstructured, it needs to go through a number of processes in order to make it suitable for use.

Data Cleansing or Data Cleaning

The data cleansing or data cleaning process is another lengthy procedure in data science. Through the cleansing and cleaning of data, corrupt and inaccurate data and datasets are corrected or removed from the database. If data is incorrect or irrelevant, it must be modified. If left in an incorrect form, this data can cause misleading or false results when analyzed. This is a vital step in data science in order to produce the highest quality results.

Data Warehouse

Data warehouses are used by businesses and organizations to store and maintain data captured from various sources. These are often relational databases that are accessed from a cloud server or mainframe server. The data stored in these warehouses is detailed, making it easy to search and analyze. While they may seem similar to database management systems, data warehouses require a deeper understanding of business intelligence software systems, data marts, data processing systems, and online analytical processing systems.

Data Staging

Data staging is simply the area where the data you are gathering is held while it waits to be extracted, transformed, cleansed, cleaned, and loaded. This may seem insignificant, but you need to know where and how to properly stage your data using different tools. If you skip out on this seemingly minor detail, you might find yourself swimming in data and datasets that are out of place and disorganized.

Data Processing

Data processing is the step that turns all the data obtained into useful and viable information. It is through data processing that the raw data collected takes on a visual appearance in the form of charts, graphs, and other documents so that employees or computer systems can easily understand the information. The data processing is done through a number of steps.

1. First, data is collected from various sources, such as data warehouses. This data must be reliable, gathered from a trustworthy source, and be of the highest quality.
2. Once the data is collected, it goes through a preparation process. During this step, the raw data is given a pre-processing cleaning to detect errors. If redundant, incorrect, incomplete, or just corrupt data is discovered, it is removed.
3. After the data has been processed, it then needs to be inputted into its designated destination, either a CRM or data warehouse. Here, the data is translated into a more understandable language.
4. Once the data has been inputted into the system, the system processes the data for interpretation. Algorithms are used to process the data in this step.
5. The processed data is then ready for output. It is during this stage where the data is transformed into its useable form.

From here, the data can be passed along and used for other analyses.

6. Once the data has been properly processed, it then goes into a storage system so it can be saved for future use. Properly storing the data is just as vital as the processing itself. Much of the data will not be used immediately but will need to be easily retrieved and accessed later.

Data Architecture

Data architecture refers to the data management plan that will provide the framework for how the data will be organized. Data architecture also involves having a clear understanding of data sources that are both internal and external, and designing a layout that will allow the data from these sources to be integrated, protected, centralized, and maintained. This is necessary for data science, as it allows team members and employees to access vital information when they need it.

Data Mining

When you have smaller data, data mining is still used in data science to finely sift through certain smaller datasets. Data mining is an effective way to find valuable data quickly and systematically.

Regression

You will hear a lot about regression when it comes to data science, mostly during the modeling phase. Regression involves taking the collected data and reducing it to utilize only the values necessary to make the most accurate prediction. In data science, regression algorithm models are some of the first implemented. While there are a number of regression models that can be considered, the five most common include:

1. Linear Regression

Linear regression makes use of linear variables. It focuses on using a model to show the relationship between the various input variables and how they work together to produce an output variable. When the model is first created, it often focuses on one independent input variable and the dependent output variable—this is referred to as a single variable linear regression. Multivariable linear regressions are created to focus on how multiple independent output variables relate to one another and the dependent output variable produced. Linear regression models are easy to program and are useful when there is not a lot of data needed, or if the relationship between the variables being modeled is not overly complicated. It can only be used, however, when only linear variables are being used.

2. Polynomial Regression

Polynomial regression models are able to input non-linear data. With this model, more than one independent variable can be included, and each variable can have exponents. These exponents can be assigned to the desired variables. In order to properly assign the exponents to the right variable, you will need to have an understanding of how these variables affect the output. If the exponents are not selected carefully, this can result in overfitting. These models are able to interpret more complex requests because they are more flexible.

3. Ridge Regression

When there is a high collinearity between the variables, a ridge regression model will be necessary. Collinearity refers to a non-linear relationship in the independent variable, which can result in the model being too restricted or rigid. A squared ridge regression or bias is added to a linear regression.

Standard linear regression ---> $\mathbf{min \, | \, Xw - y \, |^2}$

Ridge regression ---> $min \, | \, Xw - y \, |^2 + z| \, w \, |^2$

Lasso Regression

Lasso regression resembles a ridge regression, where a bias is added to optimize the desired output. Instead of adding a squared bias, however, it adds an absolute bias. We will cover what exactly a bias is in more depth and why it is used in a later chapter. For now, it is best to simply understand that a bias can be incorporated into the model design to increase an accurate probability rate or success rate.

Lasso regression ---> $\min | Xw - y |^2 + z| w |$

4.   ElasticNet Regression

ElasticNet regression is a combination of ridge regression and lasso regression.

ElasticNet Regression ---> $\min \| Xw - y \|^2 + z\_1\| w \| + z\_2\| w \|^2$

Data Clustering and Data Classification

You need to understand Data clustering and data classification as well as their differences in order to accurately classify data into clusters or groups. For this, it is important to have a clear understanding of k-means or hierarchical clustering algorithms that are used often.

Data Modeling

Data modeling is used to make predictions based on the collected data. Data models can be used for classification, forecasting, or to better understand behaviors. When modeling comes into play, machine learning and artificial intelligence are typically introduced into the data science phases.

Exploratory Data Analysis

This type of analysis is necessary to begin uncovering patterns in the data. Through exploratory data analysis, you will first investigate the raw data and use it to test the hypothesis. Here, you will begin to make sense of the data and see how it can be manipulated to gain more insight.

Confirmatory Data Analysis

The confirmatory analysis involves a more in-depth evaluation of data. Through this type of analysis, you begin to prove or disprove your assumptions though various tests and additional studies, which can produce an estimation of your predictions.

Predictive Analysis

Predictive analysis is implemented with the models you will use to test your hypothesis. This type of analysis uses statistics to predict future events or behaviors. Along with predictive analysis, you will need to be able to calculate probability, as well. A simple equation to remember to help calculate probability looks like:

$P(A)=n(E)/n(S)$

P stands for the probability of what might happen.

n(E) refers to the number of outcomes that were favorable.

n(s) is the number of possible outcomes in a set.

Key Players of a Data Science Team

As you can see, a great deal of knowledge is needed to implement data science. This is why data science projects will often have a team of professionals who specialize in various areas of data science. Most data science teams will include:

1. Data scientists

Data scientists often lead the data science team. This is because they are highly skilled at analyzing a large amount of raw data, and have the ability to process the data into useful information and identify patterns in the data. They can also help businesses utilize the information gathered from the data to make more strategic decisions to grow their operations. Data scientists have a deep understanding of many mathematical equations necessary for data science.

2. Data engineer

The data engineer is who the data scientist may rely on for making the raw data more readable. Data engineers are skilled at processing large batches of data, processing real-time data, and establishing methods to store and gather additional data.

3. Data architect

Data architects will often work with data engineers to create solutions to optimize the performances of databases, analytical applications, and frameworks.

4. Machine learning engineer

Much of the data gathered through data science is put to use for machine learning. A machine learning engineer is necessary to create models, implement algorithms, and understand the various languages, techniques, and networks used in machine learning.

5. Data analyst

Data analysts are able to transform, manipulate, and correct data for the purpose of analysis. Data analysis is common in business infrastructures, and they can be key players in understanding how certain businesses operate. This allows them to better prepare the data obtained.

Depending on the size of the company, the amount of data, and the overall goal, a data science team can consist of many more individuals who further specialize in these areas. Each of these members plays a vital role in the life cycle of the data science project. For much smaller data science teams, which is typical for startups, they may, in fact, be comprised of only a data scientist or analyst at first, with additional members added when necessary.

Data Science Life Cycle

The data science life cycle is similar to the scientific method. You initially need to identify the problem and establish a question that needs to be answered. This is the first step to take when it comes to data science. Before you begin to gather data, you need to know what data needs to be collected and analyzed. This question will be the driving force of the data science process. During this process, a majority of time is spent simply cleaning and gathering data, while only a little more than a quarter of that time is spent modeling and communicating the data. The time spent in each phase of the life cycle does not equate to its importance. Each stage is crucial to understanding and utilizes the information in the most valuable way to reach a predictable outcome.

There are a number of data science life cycles. The OSEMN data science framework breaks down the process as follows:

- Obtain
- Scrub
- Explore
- Model
- Interpret

Since there are so many smaller steps to take in data science, this is a very simplified way to reduce any intimidation. With this framework, you begin by obtaining the data, or gathering the data that you need. Then, you clean the data, also known as scrubbing, before the data is explored or visualized to detect patterns. After patterns have been detected, you can begin to create your model, which will be trained to make a specific prediction based on the data that has been explored.

After the model has been tested, you will interpret the data to evaluate the results.

While this is an easy way to explain the data science life cycle, it leaves out some key points and does not fully explain what each phase entails. What also needs to be remembered is that even if you have completed one phase successfully, that does not mean you won't need to revisit if it is discovered that additional data is needed or missing.

Another framework that includes a crucial step and also helps reduce the risk of missing out on vital data is a six-step data science life cycle.

Step 1

Before you begin any data science project, you need to first know what it is you are looking for. Many projects begin when a business or company comes to you with their own problems or questions they would like to have answered. This question or problem is similar to a hypothesis and is commonly referred to as such. This is a good starting point in formulating the focus question of the problem, but it may not be what actually needs to be solved.

When you begin a data science project, you need to fully understand the business you are doing the project for and the industry in which it operates. Once you have a clear understanding of this, you have a better understanding of how the business functions. This can provide valuable information that will assist you in determining what data to look for, where to look for that data, and what you should be gaining from that data. This is where having a clear knowledge of business intelligence comes in handy.

While the question and problems that the business hands you at the start of the project may very well be what you need to focus the project around, you need to do additional research to determine and create a clear question that will be answered from the data science project. This question will drive the workflow for the rest of the project. The question should:

1. Focus on how it can make the business more productive or operate more efficiently.
2. Focus on the business values and how the project will be able to uphold them.
3. Save the business money or bring more profit to the business.
4. Have an impact on how systems are used by the business or industry.

When you take these key points into consideration, you will create a strong question that needs to be answered.

Step 2

After you have formed your question, you will then begin to gather your data. In this step, you do not just focus on collecting the data you have available already, but you also need to consider the data you need to obtain. This step can take up a great deal of time but is one of the most crucial steps. Without the right data, the rest of the project will not run as smoothly, and you won't be able to answer the question from step one successfully.

When gathering data, you will need to consider all the sources you have at your disposal, the type of data that is coming from these sources, and if there are sources that you need to investigate to gather more data from. While some projects will only need a small amount of data—and this will depend on the question you are answering—many other projects may require a great deal more data than you can simply pull from a company's database.

You will need to know how to precisely search through large databases, retrieve data from web API systems, and understand various programming frameworks. Conducting data searches is a skill that is typically perfected the more you do it, so while it may take a great deal of time for you to retrieve the right data for your first few projects, you will feel more confident and be able to do this at a faster rate with each new initiative.

Step 3

The third step is also time-consuming. In fact, most of your data science project's time is spent in the second and third steps. This phase will require you to thoroughly examine all the data you have obtained and clean it. Since a great deal of the data you collect will most likely be unstructured, it will often not be perfect. Much of the data will have missing variables, be poorly formatted, or completely useless.

Here, you need to implement the "garbage in, garbage out" process for filtering data that is relevant and irrelevant. The goal of this phase is to consolidate all data into one format in order to easily analyze it. Only the necessary data is kept and organized to be used in the next phase. This can be done with little effort when the data is structured, but when data is unstructured, it needs to be converted to a format that will allow further actions and analysis to be conducted.

This is also a vital step because if any pieces of the data are missing or incorrect, the modeling step will not go smoothly. You have to ensure that the data you use from here to the end of the project is of the highest quality; otherwise, you will not have the most accurate results. You have to take the time and do this with all the data that is collected.

Luckily, there are some tools that can help make this process go a little faster. Hadoop, Mapreduce, Spark, and Python are different tools that can help with data mining, scrubbing, and scripting.

Step 4

In step four, you begin to transform the data into valuable information. This is also where having a clearly outlined question will be helpful. During this step, you will first begin to categorize your data. As you will learn in Chapter 3, data can fall into several categories. The more specifically you can label, organize, and define your data, the better you will be able to analyze it.

This phase will involve a great deal of calculation to determine if there are disturbances in the datasets or deviation noticed. Calculating the mean, median, and mode of the data collected is often a starting point in exploring data. Not all data will allow you to calculate each of these components; some, you may only be able to find the mode, others just the medium.

Begin able to extract the statistical values and find the connection between the variables will have an impact on how you test your data and set up your model for testing. Here, you need to know which characteristics of the data will have the biggest impact on the outcome or how will it help solve the problem. You will need to test and analyze specific variables to gain a deeper insight into their impact.

In this step, you will also have visuals that show the relevance of your data. This visualization will better demonstrate the patterns, trends, flaws, and importance of the data. These visualizations are typically some variation or combination of charts, graphs, and tables.

Step 5

Step five is typically the more eagerly anticipated phase, though there is still a great deal of work, testing, and experimentation that needs to be done. During step five, you will create a model that will test out the hypothesis based on the problem you are trying to solve. Through all your data analysis and calculation, you should be able to understand where or what needs to be done differently in order for the business to yield more significant results either in productivity, financially, or systematically.

During this step, you will implement the use of a machine learning model or a deep learning model. This will also be discussed in further detail in later chapters. But, before you can begin to develop your model, you need to have clear data sets and a well-organized plan for testing and training. This is also where you will learn whether or not you have done an adequate job at gathering, cleaning, and scrubbing your data.

From the data you have to use for the modeling phase, you want to ensure that only the most relevant and data sets are used. What features, values and contributions are vital for the success of your outcome? You want to select only the relevant data sets that will have the most influence of the predictive outcome as entering the data, testing the model, and training the model can take a great deal of time, and you may not have much time available.

This stage will also require you to cluster your data with relevant data points to help make a more logical sense of the information. Algorithms, calculations, and various methods will be used throughout this process. These will also be implemented by the model you plan to train. Modeling is where machine learning becomes a predominant component. This is where you need to understand how to optimize your model, make a projection model, perform predictive analytics, and then create a classic model.

You will begin to train your machine learning or deep learning model to perform basic classification in order to determine the accuracy and performance. How this is done will be covered in greater detail when we discuss the neural networks and parameters of machine learning and deep learning. This is where you will see if the machine can make an accurate prediction based on the data you have collected, and if these predictions will allow it to help solve the company problem you are focusing on.

Step 6

After the modeling has been tested, many spend the remainder of the project life cycle analyzing their results. You want to be able to determine how successful your efforts were. This will require using various calculations and classifications to measure your findings, such as:

- F1 score
- Mean Average Error, or MAE
- Root Mean Square, or RMSE

The most valuable insights you can gain from your results are actionable insights. These not only show the effectiveness of your research, but also show others how they can easily implement steps, tools, or procedures to generate the same outcomes in their own businesses. Being able to accurately predict future events for a business in a way that shows how they benefit from your findings is what makes your data science project successful.

Aside from evaluating your results, you want to be able to ensure the business can put these findings to use. A critical process in this final step is drafting your data reports and creating a compelling presentation. In the last chapter of this book, you will see why this is such a crucial component in the data science project and how you can utilize this often-skipped component to better show your results and bring attention to the impact the research can have. Communication is a skill that most do not develop enough to effectively present their finding, but it is vital in this process.

During this final step, all the data and work you have done to create models, organize, analyze, and make predictions will either be viewed as useful or confusion. Here, you will not only calculate the success of your results, but you will also be able to present your models and data in a way that should invoke action to be taken to achieve the desired outcome.

Core Components of Data Science

While there are many elements that go into data science, its three core components are necessary to understand in order to undertake a successful data science project. Even if you begin with just one data point, having an understanding of these core components will allow you to create, test, and validate a model to explain that data point. Data scientists tend to have an extensive understanding of each of these core components that drive data science.

1. Domains and Business Knowledge

Artificial intelligence is a key component of data science. While many have a misunderstanding of what artificial intelligence actually entails, much of it is used regularly in data science. Artificial intelligence also helps data scientists make predictions about future events. Machine learning is one subset of artificial intelligence that is popular among data scientists. When it comes to domain and business knowledge, artificial intelligence is one of the most effective tools businesses are using to gather data. In order to create an AI system, you need to have an understanding of the domain or business it is going to be used on and for.

2. Computer Science and IT

You not only need to have an understanding of database management system, but also a clear understanding of various algorithms. These algorithms are used throughout the data science life cycles. Algorithms are used to detect patterns in the data, machine learning models, and classification systems. Aside from the algorithms, a data scientist needs to have a strong understanding of programming systems. Some of the most common computer programming tools used in data science include Oracle, R, Python, and C++.

3. Math and Statistics

In data science, a comprehensive knowledge of mathematics and statistics is vital for structuring machine learning models and neural networks. While algorithms can be used to retrieve data and set expectations for the machine model, you will have to understand how to figure out how many components of certain features need to be added. Some basic math calculations you may find yourself doing frequently involve calculating the mean, median, or mode of data sets. Additionally, you may need to have a clear understanding of more complex linear algebra examples. You will also have to learn both business and applied statistics.

The Future of Data Science

The introduction of the internet and smartphones has led to an increase in available data, which, in turn, results in an increase in the application of data science across every industry. As more individuals begin and continue to experiment with artificial intelligence and advanced machine learning, the need to fully understand and implement the necessary components of data science will be more and more important.

Data scientists have grown to be a highly in-demand professional and are scarce. With technology constantly changing and advancing, data science will see significant growth, as the amount of data being made available also grows. Specific roles, skills, and education of data science areas will evolve and change for many years.

Since data science is still relatively new, very few individuals can consider themselves experts in the field. As such, there is still much that can be discovered about these areas, and the specific roles of those involved in data science are still being defined. In this sense, data science has a great deal more expanding to do, even though it has quickly changed the world in just a few short years.

Another thing to keep in mind when it comes to data science is the versatility of data itself. Since data science is at the root of many new technological systems and advancement, it can confidently be assumed that as long as technology continues to evolve and change, data science can be expected to follow the same footsteps.

Chapter 2
Understanding Big Data

"Every day, three times per second, we produce the equivalent of the amount of data that the Library of Congress has in its entire print collection, right? But most of it is like, cat videos on YouTube, or 13-year-olds exchanging text messages about the next Twilight movie."

-Nate Silver, founder of FiveThirtyEight

What is Big Data?

Big data refers to a large quantity of structured and unstructured data. This is used when traditional methods for extracting value from data sets becomes futile. When the data sets become too big to analyze, more advanced and sophisticated tools, systems, and techniques need to be on-boarded to make use of this data. While many believe too much data can harm their system, in fact, the more data is collected, the more insight you can gain. Big data is distinguished by:

- Velocity
- Variety
- Volume
- Value
- Veracity

It is not just the amount of data that is considered. Big data also includes many different types of data that flows in at an incredibly fast rate, which is readily available in real-time. The data also must be of value, which means it must contain information allowing for new insight to be discovered or to be used in ways never possible before.

For businesses, this is especially vital because advanced technology is making it easier than ever to access this wide variety of data in order to drive their businesses forward. Businesses are beginning to realize that it isn't enough to just gather more data—they need to be able to understand what this data means. With such a high volume, however, many companies are not taking full advantage of all they can uncover and the insight they can gain from this big data that can significantly impact the growth of their operations.

Unfortunately, data is collected and stored and little is ever done with it because all that can be done is not fully understood. Big data was the key motivator behind data science, as the approaches used in data science revolve around deciphering large amounts of data. But companies have had always collected and stored data and have a massive amount of data stored in databases. Big data and databases are two different entities—while many companies can have large databases, they can also obtain big data.

How does big data differ from the database?

It is understandable how databases and big data can be confused, as they seem to refer to the same things. Both involve large amounts of data, but there is a major difference between the two. Big data encompasses all types and forms of data. Databases, on the other hand, refers to where data is stored. Databases can be used to store big data, but that does not mean the database itself is considered big data. Databases are simply the structures used to store data. Big data could be what is being stored. While they may seem to be similar, databases and big data are two different elements of data science.

You can have a lot of data stored in databases, but big data tends to refer more toward the amount of data that flows in from multiple sources over a concise amount of time, as opposed to databases, which store a lot of data sets which have been collected over a specific period of time.

Big Data Frameworks

Because of the amount of data that is being produced in a short amount of time, big data needs unique systems and tools to help process, store, analyze, capture, search, share, query, update, transfer, and secure these large quantities of data. Special frameworks have been designed to help utilize big data with more ease, speed, and efficiency.

Parallel systems are often necessary to process big data faster and analyzing it more accurate. A parallel system and parallel computing system allow for big data to be accessed by multiple users while permitting searches, management, analysis, and more to be done simultaneously through one framework. For businesses, these parallel servers and software systems allow for more data to be inputted—not just from workers but from the user as well.

The most commonly used big data frameworks include:

Apache Hadoop and MapReduce

Apache Hadoop is a popular open-source software. It allows anyone who understands data processing to use the system, and operates by utilizing two components:

1. HDFS, which focuses on storing data into clusters.
2. MapReduce, which focuses on calculating and processing the data in a cluster.

Hadoop can identify new data sources, cutting back on time it would typically take to notice or uncover them. As a result, decisions can be made quicker based on new data collected in real-time, which can often help identify emerging trends. MapReduce and Hadoop work together to provide instant 'Cliff Notes' of data from its server. This big data framework is an easy way to search a table of content like systems, to search for data and to find the specific server it is coming from. The data is stored or saved on a hard drive.

Apache Storm

Apache Storm focuses on the data flow of big data. It is equipped with scalable features allowing for the fast processing and distribution of cluster data. It also has vital tools that make it stand out from other analog systems. It utilizes tuple, a data representation element with the ability to incorporate the serialization of data. Stream is the tool that helps make the fields in tuple. Data is received through Spout, which activates the development of tuples from this external data and then sends it to Stream. These tools, along with the data processor, Bolt and Topology, allow for an endless amount of unstructured data to flow the processing phases.

Apache Hive

Apache Hive also uses the MapReduce tool, along with SQL. It is more of an engine that allows for big data to be sorted, optimize, and outputted for specific tasks throughout the MapReduce framework. The Apache Hive engines can easily be integrated with Apache Hadoop and work seamlessly with MapReduce for a more efficient way to analyze large quantities of data.

Apache Spark

Another open-source framework to consider using big data is Apache Spark. This framework was specially designed to work with big data and therefore has a number of more advanced features when compared to Hadoop. Apache Spark uses a random-access memory, which allows it to perform significantly faster when retrieving data. This framework consists of five basic structures—one is the core of the system, along with four big data libraries. These libraries include:

- Spark SQL for structured data
- Spark library, which features a streaming tool that allows for real-time data processing
- MLib library, dedicated to machine learning systems

- GraphX for scalable processing of data in graph form

Big Data Cloud-Based Analytics

Cloud-based systems have also been created as a big data solution. These systems are highly effective for big corporations or enterprises to use to store all the data they retrieve on a daily basis. Cloud-based systems have been around for years, but private sectors have been mostly used. Now, with innovative tools, more public systems are being favored. Many companies are taking advantage of a hybrid system that will allow them to eventually make a smoother transition into a fully public cloud system over the next few years. Developers are constantly finding ways to streamline big data applications that will allow for big data analytics to be run with less time and more efficiency. With more sophisticated data science tools, cloud-based big data databases are equipped with services and pre-trained models that can be customized and transitioned into business infrastructures as an optimal business solution.

Data Science, Big Data, and Data Analysis? What are Their Roles?

Data science, big data, and data analysis tend to be used as interchangeable terms. While each of these are interlinked, they all possess fundamentals and features that separate them. Each is used in connection with one another to have a more significant impact on business operations and industry standards and solutions.

Data science is the approach taken when dealing with big data. Through data science, big data can be processed using more advanced tools, mathematical solutions, and statistical ideas. Because of big data, data science has evolved into a highly specialized area. Without big data, there would be no need for data science, since traditional methods are able to easily perform tasks needed to gain insight from smaller quantities of data.

Data analysis is a process of data science where data is cleaned, processed, transformed, and analyzed. The analytics of data science refers to the methods used to understand data gathered in order to make better decisions. Data analysis tests the hypothesis data science is trying to solve through modeling based on specific data sets.

Data analysis is a diverse category that can incorporate different approaches for analyzing data.

1. Descriptive Analysis

Descriptive analysis gives the first glimpse of insight into the collected data. This type of data analysis is the most widely used in businesses, as it serves an easy way to track past performances. Descriptive analysis is used to uncover what happened in the past, which may have an impact on what happens in the future. This is used in revenue reports or when tracking key performance indicators of a business.

2. Diagnostic Analysis

Diagnostic analysis piggybacks off the information gathered through the descriptive analysis, taking into consideration the information previously discovered and diving deeper to learn why things happened. With diagnostic analysis, patterns are being detected and more details are being extracted from the data. Diagnostic analysis can uncover the 'why' factor to a problem, such as why shipments are slow or which marketing campaigns are more successful than others.

3. Predictive Analysis

Predictive analysis makes a prediction based on information gathered through descriptive and diagnostic analysis. This is a more challenging type of data analysis. With predictive analysis, statistical modeling comes into play. This is where more advanced technologies are required and clear, detailed, quality data is needed to ensure the predictions forecasted are as accurate as possible.

4. Prescriptive Analysis

Finally, once a prediction has been formulated based on the data analyzed, an action plan is drafted. Prescriptive analysis is used to show what steps need to be taken to solve the current problem. The solutions prescriptive analysis points to are often artificial intelligent systems such as machine learning or deep learning models. These models are able to automate or streamline areas of the workflow to yield more favorable results and be implemented as highly innovative business solutions.

While big data, data science, and data analysis work together, they each exhibit distinct roles in the ever-changing world of technology. Big data is a massive amount of various data generated through different sources. Data science is the way companies and industries make sense of this data. Data analysis is one of the many tools used in data science to extract deeper insight into the mounds of big data.

Chapter 3
What is Data?

"You can have data without information, but you cannot have information without data."

-Daniel Keys Moran

Data Defined

Data can come in a variety of forms, and can be obtained from multiple sources. What is considered data can range from colors present in an image to the age of a new customer. Information collected from a website in terms of views, visits, and navigation are also some forms of data. This can be visual, numerical, text, models, variables, videos, and sounds, or any set of characters.

Because data can come in such diverse forms, it needs to be organized systematically. Data is organized by data sets. A data set consists of specific variables and lists the values associated with these variables. Data sets can also include files or documents and can be formulated by algorithms, which can be used for software testing. Data types have an impact on the variables you discover, as well as the tools you use to analyze it.

Where to Find Data

The most common place to find data now is online. Various websites are already set up to track specific data sets that can be easily downloaded. The following sites are worth exploring when you are looking for reliable data:

1. Data.world

Data.world offers a number of useful features for data science projects. Not only can you find a wide range of data sets for use, but you can also upload your own data sets to gain feedback and insight from other users. Additionally, this site allows you to access copy, analyze, and create your own SQL queries to make it easier to organize and explore various data sets.

2. Kaggle

Kaggle is one of the well-known repositories for machine learning data. The sites focus on hosting various machine learning competitions, which is how you can access a great deal of the data sets available. You can easily download the data sets, which are externally submitted— some of them may not be of the best quality, and will have to be clean and scrubbed to get the most use out of them. For beginners, this can be a great place to start for a better understanding of how to use data for specific machine learning purposes.

3. FiveThirtyEight

FiveThirtyEight has a number of data sets available through their own sites and Github. Most of the data sets you will find are centered around data journalism. The articles they publish on their site also offer insight into statistics. Some of the information you can gather from this site includes historical details, such as previous weather conditions for certain areas, drug studies based primarily in the United States, and accident reports from airplanes.

4. Data.gov

To obtain government data, data.gov is where you want to search first. Through this source, you can obtain a wide range of data covering crime rates to climate change. You can also access information about populations, education, and additional information concerning the

U.S. population. Thought the site does offer significant data sets, it can be more confusing to navigate than many of the other options you have available. You may also be required to agree to different licensing terms and conditions before you are granted permission to download the data set. These terms and conditions can include restrictions on how the data can be used, which is something you will want to carefully read over prior to using the data.

5. Quandl

Quandl offers more in-depth data in the specific areas of finance and the economy. The data is ideal for machine learning, and because of the quantity of data available, it is even possible to complete a full model from the data set.

6. UCI machine repository

Another repository that focuses on machine learning data is the UCI Machine Learning Repository. As one of the oldest data sources you can find, the data sets tend to be smaller and can be downloaded directly from the site. You will need to thoroughly check the data sets for quality, as a number of them are from user contributions. Some of the data you can gather from UCI machine learning repository include those that focus on email use, such as spam mail, or attributes of products, such as wine. This is a great place to start your data search as you may find some interesting data sets that you might not have considered.

7. Academic torrents

Academic torrents offer a unique library of data. A majority of the data you can find is based on academic papers and previously conducted research. For example, you can gather data on how email is used in different companies such as Enron, the factors that affect student learning, or the number of news articles that cover a specific topic. The data sets offer a different perspective on some interesting topics. These data sets can be quite large, but can be downloaded directly from the site if you are a BitTorrent client.

8. Buzzfeed

You may have rolled your eyes at this one. Buzzfeed is well known for some questionable content, but this isn't the case when it comes to their data journalism. In this category, their information and data fall into the same high-quality realm as FiveThirtyEight—and just like FiveThirtyEight, their data sets are publicly available through Github, as well. Some examples of the data you can make use of through Buzzfeed include information on federal surveillance or virus outbreaks, and data regarding various background checks such as those conducted for firearm purchases.

9. Google

Google has a number of different sources and tools for public access to obtain data that revolves around trends, finances, books, keywords, and more. It offers one of the widest varieties of different types of data covering a number of topics.

10. GitHub

GitHub offers a range of useful information tools and samples that include different machine learning, deep learning and data methods. You can find a large amount of data that covers coding, from the quality score to the evolution. You can access this data from an API on GitHub.

But data does not just refer to what is found on the internet. Data can be retrieved from just about anywhere. What one must understand is that while data can be retrieved from many sources, this does not always result in useful data. Only through an in-depth exploration of this data or data set can the information it contains be uncovered. This is what data science accomplishes.

Types of Data

What needs to be clearly understood is that your data affects the methods, tools, and processes you need to implement through your data science project. Each data has its own use and will provide you with different values and insights.

Unstructured Data

Unstructured data makes up a majority of the available data. This data can be human-generated or computer-generated and, while it has an internal structure, it does not have a predetermined model or schema that it can easily into. If data does not fall into the structured or semi-structured category, it lands in the unstructured form of data.

Unstructured data is more challenging to analyze for big data use but it is the most commonly used data for machine learning and to better understand customers. Unstructured data is also referred to as qualitative data, since it is mostly opinions or judgments.

Semi-Structured Data

Semi-structured data makes up the smallest amount of data available. This data has tags and classification that allows it to be grouped in hierarchies, but can be manipulated or changed. Prime examples of semi-structured data are email, XML, or JavaScript.

Structured Data

Structured data is easy to search and analyze. It consists of defined patterns and data types. Structured data is often found in relational databases or RDBMS. Structured data is referred to as quantitative data, since it shows facts and real numbers.

Data sets

Aside from these three basic types of data, you will find more specific data types sub-categories. These are often more effectively labels and classified as data sets. These include:

Categorical data: This data focus on the characteristics of the data that do not present any mathematical meanings. Examples of categorical data types include gender, language, demographics.

Nominal data: Nominal data labels variables. This data also provides no quantitative value.

Ordinal data: Ordinal data is similar to nominal data, except that the units used to label the variables cannot be changed in the order it is presented. An example of this type of data would be determining the level of education someone has completed. The levels of education need to be listed in a specific order, i.e., from the lowest level of education to the highest level. This type of data is often used to understand data that has no numerical scale of measurements, such as customer satisfaction or employee happiness.

Numerical data: Data that can be measured will fall into numerical data. Numerical data can be either discrete or continuous.

Discrete data: Discrete data has very distinct and categorized values. This data can be counted, but not measured.

Continuous data: Continuous data is the opposite of discrete data, where it can be measured but not counted. This data can often be classified using intervals based on real number values.

Interval data: This data is represented by organized units, where the difference from one unit to the next is equal. An example of this would be when determining the temperature for a location and you are presented with temperatures from lowest to highest, with an increase of 5 degrees (-10, -5, 0, 5, 10). This type of data is easy to add or subtract but is not useful to calculate specific ratios. This is data that can be valuable for descriptive or statistical information.

How to Use Data?

The way you use the collected data will be a process of placing the data into its appropriate categories. In order to obtain a deeper insight into this information, data science uses specialized tools to further examine and classify data. After separating your structured, unstructured, and semi-structured data, you will first need to determine whether the data has quantitative or qualitative value, or whether it can be measured or whether it can be observed. The second thing you need to do to categorize your data labels it as either continuous or discrete for quantitative data, or if the data is qualitative, as binomial, nominal, or ordinal. When the data is discrete, the value is precisely known, while if it is continuous, the values can be reduced or made more precise such as with measurement of length. Continuous data is useful when formulating hypothesis tests. Binomial information is data that contains two structured categories, such as right/wrong, good/bad. Nominal data is the qualitative data that is categorized in a way where they are not true value, such as color. Ordinal data can be categorized in a way where the natural value is important, such as going from short to tall in height.

When data can be broken down into more specific categories, it can be better analyzed and understood. In data science, the primary use of data is as a form of information. Data that is gathered is thoroughly examined for its value. This is especially important for businesses. Data collected can be used to understand buying trends, needs, and expectations. Businesses are better able to cater to their audiences in a way that improves customer relations, shopping experiences, and value, which results in an increase in profit and customer retention.

Satisfying customers isn't the only way data is being used. More and more, businesses are using data to improve workflow, productivity, efficiency, and team collaboration. Data has been a crucial component in determining where weak links can be found in their systems. For businesses, being able to analyze data precisely can reduce costs and increase quality in their services and products. Only when the data is properly examined can the real value of it be determined.

Chapter 4
Machine Learning

"People worry that computers will get too smart and take over the world, but the real problem is that they're too stupid and they've already taken over the world."

-Pedro Domingos, author

What is Machine Learning?

Machine learning is a subset of artificial intelligence. It focuses on the application and capabilities of computers to access and learn from data. Data is first observed to identify patterns from which the machine should be able to make future predictions based on the data sample provided. The process used to observe this data is known as data science. The goal is to train a model to perform appropriate actions without human interference, or at least with minimal assistance.

A common type of machine learning is progressive learning, which many online servers implement. This type of learning allows new data to be obtained and updated continuously. Here, the machine is able to learn, label, and classify data when new information is obtained. An example of this type of machine learning is used when predicting stock prices.

The main goals of any type of machine learning are:

1. To make predictions

Machines are trained through data to make future predictions of specific events. The data used is the key to the machine learning how to make accurate predictions.

2. To identify patterns

Machines can also be trained to recognize different patterns in the data. From the examples it is fed, it is able to determine what should occur, based on the similarities extracted from the data samples.

The Basic Fundamentals of Machine Learning

1. Data preparation

The data preparation step of machine learning is one of the most time-consuming phases. Data needs to be carefully assessed and analyzed, so only the most relevant and useful information is collected. Since much of the data may be unstructured, the process is complicated—most data will have missing or incorrect variables, be poorly formatted, or need to have more content generated in order to be used for specific machine learning models.

This process is vital, however, because data sets need to be created to meet the specifications of the algorithms used. If any of the data is missing, incorrect, or incomplete, the algorithms will not be able to use the data properly. When extra time is taken to carefully prepare the data, you will achieve more accurate and practical results in the testing and training phase.

Through your data prep, you want to be able to visualize that data, as well as draw statistics from it. You also want to understand what feature engineering requirements will be necessary to take the raw data and transform it into data that can be used in the model. Feature engineering can help the model interpret data, capture complex relationships, reduce redundancy or dimensionality, and reliable variables.

Some machine learning models will feature different engineering requirements. But you will need to know exactly what you need the machine to do with the data used in order to determine which of these features will be a necessity.

2. Algorithms

There are a number of algorithms to choose from in machine learning, which will have a direct impact on how effectively the model will learn and process data. When choosing an algorithm, you want to take into consideration these key factors:

- *Know the problem.* Many algorithms are designed to solve specific problems. By first understanding the problem you want to solve, you will be able to better determine which algorithm is best suited to the task.
- *Set the size of your training sets.* The size of your set will impact which algorithm is most effective at processing and transforming the data into learnable information. Smaller sets benefit from algorithms that implement high bias and low variance classifiers. Larger data sets will require algorithms that have a low bias high variance classifier because a high bias with more training sets will typically yield inaccurate results.
- *How accurate the results need to be.* Algorithms can be used to produce varying results, which can often be just an approximation. Setting approximation can often lead to shorter processing times and can result in overfitting.
- *How much time is needed to complete the training.* Each algorithm will have its own time restraints, so you need to have a clear idea of how much time can be dedicated to training. This can be easily estimated by considering the size of the data sets to be used and what the target accuracy is. Knowing these two factors will allow you to choose the appropriate algorithm that can achieve the goal in a given amount of time.

- *Know your parameters.* This is discussed in more detail in Chapter 7, but needs to be mentioned when choosing your algorithms. Parameters have an effect on how much time is needed for training, and testing out parameters separately is another consideration that needs to be addressed. The more the parameters, the more time it will take to find the right combination of parameters and get the model to yield accurate results.
- *What features the model needs to possess to achieve the desired goal.* Each machine learning model can be used with various algorithms, but some have limits on which can be used. Models can have varying levels of complexities. Some models need only a few features to learn or predict a specific task, while others will require a number of features to meet the target output. The more features, the more algorithms you may need to use with that model. Excessive features can also slow down the learning process and have a negative impact on the training time.

3. Automation Iterative Processes

Since the data used for machine learning is quite large, data sets are often broken down into smaller batches. Setting up a system that allows for the automation of large data sets to be fed through the machine automatically can save a great deal of time. Additionally, in order to get the most accurate results from machine learning, data needs to be fed through the machine a number of times. Each time the data is fed through the machine, it is also provided with the results from the previous feed. Thus, the machine is able to identify the flaws it made in previous calculations to make better predictions with the current data feed. This process results in the machine using the algorithm to fine-tune results and, therefore, the probability of reaching the optimal results becomes more likely. Iterative is a frequently used term in machine learning and deep learning, so you want to have a clear understanding of what it refers to.

Iterative, when used with machine learning, is the process in which data is fed repeatedly through the machine processing system. Each time it is fed the data, the calculation or predictions the machine outputs should come closer to the desired expected outcome.

4. Scalability

Scalability algorithms allow the machine to process an unlimited amount of data without using unnecessary resources, such as memory. These algorithms result in a fast computation of much larger data sets. Here, algorithms are used in new models in which the system is meant to be scaled. Machine learning models that are easily scalable can be highly successful, as they can be tweaked and adjusted to be used throughout various departments or to improve systems within the company or across industries.

5. Ensemble Modeling

Ensemble learning refers to the training of multiple models, which are then combined to improve outcomes. Each model brings its own algorithms to be implemented into one predictive model. These types of models tend to yield more accurate results and offer a higher performance quality. The downside is that each model needs to be trained on its own, then combined and trained together with the final model.

Machine Learning Algorithms

Algorithms can be organized by their learning styles or by the similar functions they perform. In machine learning, algorithms are used in order for the model to learn how to perform the expected results. These algorithms allow researchers and scientists to make adjustments in order to improve performance. The type of algorithm used depends ultimately on what the end goal is, as previously discussed. The following are some common machine learning algorithms that you can access:

Regression Algorithms

Regression is often classified as both an algorithm and a problem. Instead of just using an algorithm to train a model, this is a full process. With this method, a measure of error is implemented to show the learning rate of the model, and refinements are then made to improve this measure of error. Here, the model focuses on how the variable of the data relates to one another. An example would be calculating the time to travel from one location to another, predicting sales of a specific product for future months, or how an increase in sales of a particular product can increase revenue for the year. The most common regression algorithms include:

- Logistic Regression
- Linear Regression
- Stepwise Regression
- Ordinary Least Squares Regression, or OLSR
- Multivariate Adaptive Regression Splines, or MARS
- Locally Estimated Scatterplot Smoothing, or LOESS

Instance-Based Algorithms/Winner-Take-All Algorithms/Memory-Based Learning

With these types of algorithms, the model is trained by building up its own database of examples to solve problems. When a new data is inputted, the model recalls its database to locate similarities to measure the new data. From these measurements, the model can then make its predictions. The most common instance-based algorithms include:

- k-Nearest Neighbor, or kNN
- Locally Weighted Learning, or LWL
- Learning Vector Quantization, or LVQ
- Self Organized Map, or SOM
- Support Vector Machine, or SVMs

Regularization Algorithms

Regularized algorithms are often used in connection with other methods. Typically, a regularization algorithm can be added to a regression algorithm in order to improve the model's ability to generalize data. The most common regularization algorithms include:

- Elastic Net
- Least Absolute Shrinkage and Selection Operator, or LASSO
- Least-Angle Regression, or LARS
- Ridge Regression

Clustering Algorithms

Clustered algorithms are used to organize data based on the internal structure. The model is required to identify the problem and methods used to group data based on their most prominent similarities. The most common cluster algorithms include:

- Expectation-Maximization, or EM
- Hierarchical Clustering
- k-Means
- k-Medians

Association Rule Learning Algorithms

With association rule algorithms, the model extracts rules from the input information to explain how the variables in the data relate to one another. This is a useful model for multidimensional datasets. Many organizations benefit from these algorithms. The most common association rule learning algorithms include:

- Apriori
- Eclat algorithms

Ensemble Algorithms

Ensemble algorithms are powerful algorithms where weaker models are created and used cohesively to come up with a final accurate prediction. With these algorithms, each weaker model is trained individually, then added to a larger overall model to work in conjunction with the weaker models. The most common ensemble algorithms include:

- AdaBoost
- Boosting
- Bootstrapped Aggregation of Bagging
- Gradient Boosting Machines, or GBM
- Gradient Boosted Regression Trees, or GBRT
- Random Forest
- Stacked Generalization, or Stacking
- Weighted Average, or Blending

Types of Machine Learning

Supervised

An example of this type of learning is being able to detect whether an email is spam. Through the training process, the model is expected to make predictions. When the model makes an inaccurate prediction, it is corrected. In a supervised learning model, logistic regression and backpropagation algorithms are frequently used.

Unsupervised

With unsupervised learning, the data and results are unspecified. With this learning method, the model is most often required to organize the data, reduce redundancy, discover general rules, or locate structures present in the input. Apriori and K-Means algorithms are favored for this type of learning model.

Semi-Supervised

Semi-supervised machine learning models offer a combination of supervised and unsupervised machine learning. The data is often a cluster of labeled and unlabeled information, the model is expected to predict the desired result and identify structure in the data to organize it. The algorithms used with this type of machine learning are usually an extension of algorithms already in use, based on the model's accuracy rate.

Reinforcement

With this type of machine learning, a reinforcement signal is used as feedback to teach the model which action it implements is the best. Here, the model interacts with its surroundings to utilize a series of trial-and-error searches to determine which characteristics are the most appropriate for optimal performance. Reinforcement learning uses algorithms to choose the best action the model should take.

Machine Learning Languages and Machine Learning Software

Two main components of machine learning that need clarification are the languages and software available. Machine learning languages refers to the software system that can basically help write the machine learning algorithms for you. While you can type each algorithm and calculation manually, using a machine learning language simplifies and greatly speeds up the process.

Machine learning software assists in the full or partial process of developing a machine learning model. These software systems often work with one of the top machine learning languages, so much of the time-consuming and mundane tasks can be done for you. Many software systems can help with data prep, analysis, algorithms, setting parameters; come equipped with libraries, and can even give you feedback on the effectiveness of algorithms used.

Machine Learning Languages

1. Python

Python is a simple language that is widely used among beginner and veteran developers alike. One of the key benefits of this programming language is that it is easy to implement and comes equipped with a number of powerful tools and libraries. Pybrain is specifically designed for machine learning, and Numpy is a python library that houses solutions to scientific computation.

2. R

R is not just a programming language; it comes with a variety of packages to be specifically used for machine learning. The R language is ideal for the manipulation of data, analysis, and solving a number of statistical calculations. The R language is also a useful tool for k-nearest algorithms, which are some of the best algorithms for pattern recognition and classification.

3. Java

The Java language focuses on machine learning algorithms and neural network development. This language features a vast array of debugging tools and graphic representation and can be easily integrated with large-scale projects through an easy-to-navigate system. It is a sophisticated language that also supplies high tech tools to make machine learning a more simplified process.

4. Prolog

Prolog is a widely used language for AI systems, especially those in the medical field. The language is highly flexible, with pattern detection, data structuring, and backtracking. This language is strongly rooted in logic language programming.

5. Lisp

Lisp has been a popular AI language for years. Its key functions are its prototyping capabilities with new object creation features, while also effectively ridding the systems of garbage. Though many other languages offer similar features, Lisp's long history makes it one of the best-suited languages for machine learning.

6. C++

C++ may not be the most talked-about machine learning language but is supported by most software programs like Tensorflow. While it may be overlooked, this machine learning language is one of the oldest languages available. It offers users an easy-to-use design that can create flow graphs and perform other functional tasks.

Machine Learning Software/Frameworks

1. SciKit Learn

SciKit learning is a machine learning framework that works excellently with Python. This system offers a number of data mining and analytical tools. It offers a Python library that holds a number of algorithms for classification, regression, clustering and model selection, to point out a few. Each of the parameters attached to the algorithms can be adjusted through an easy-to-follow system.

2. Tensorflow

Tensorflow is another highly popular framework used for machine learning with JavaScript. The easily accessible APIs assist in machine learning model development, and users can also convert existing models into the system. If you don't have an existing model, you can create, train, and set up neural networks. While this is a powerful framework, it is one of the more challenging programs to learn, unless you already have an extensive understanding of machine learning and neural networks.

3. PyTorch

PyTorch is a hybrid framework that collaboratively works with Torch and Python. It offers a Python library while implementing a Lua-inspired framework and scripting language. Through this software, you can build neural networks through various algorithms and modules. PyTorch can be transitioned to cloud-based servers, as well, making it even more accessible. You can also take advantage of the additional libraries, tools, and training through the cloud-based system.

4. Weka

Weka is a specially-designed software for data mining in Java language. Students and those newer to machine learning can benefit from this software, which helps with a great deal of the data prep process, classification of data, and visualization. While it doesn't offer much in online support, it is one of the easier to learn programs with training courses available.

5. Colab

Colab is Google's cloud-based machine learning software server. It is designed to work with Python and includes a number of libraries ideal for machine learning. It also works in connection with TensorFlow, Keras, and PyTorch applications for more advanced machine learning options.

6. Keras

Keras is a popular neural network software that uses Python language. It supports some of the most common neural networks, such as convolution, recurrent, and a hydric of these two networks. To utilize the neural network features, you need to run Keras along with another framework, like TensorFlow. The platform, however, is great for creating prototypes quickly.

7. Rapid Miner

Rapid Miner is a highly advanced platform for machine learning. It also has deep learning capabilities, along with strong data prep, data mining, and analytical processes. Through Rapid Miner, you can research data, gain more knowledge around that data, and apply this to your machine development applications. The advanced machine learning features include model validation and optimization. Though this is an advanced platform, it is incredibly user-friendly and even those with the slightest understanding of machine learning will be able to easily navigate and make use of its features. The only setback to this platform is that it requires you to sign up with a plan, which can be quite pricey.

How does Machine Learning Relate to Data Science?

When data science is used to analyze data, the most common solution to business problems is found through machine learning. But the data needs to be concise for the machine to perform optimally. If any of the data collections, cleaning and classifying steps on data science are poorly conducted, the success of a machine learning solution is unlikely.

Machine learning is a core component of data science, which is used in data modeling. The machine learning model used will depend on the type of data being inputted, as well as the central question that needs to be answered. Machine learning requires a great deal of data analysis in order to deliver accurate results in the least amount of time. With the use of data science, machines are able to process large amounts of data to improve performance and achieve optimal results.

Chapter 5
Deep Learning

"As one Google Translate engineer put it, when you go from 10,000 training examples to 10 billion training examples, it all starts to work. Data trumps everything."

-Garry Kasparov

What is Deep Learning?

Deep learning is a way to use data to teach computers how to perform tasks in the same way that humans learn. It utilizes both data sets and neural networks to achieve this. This highly specialized division of machine learning can continually be improved upon as more data is inputted. Deep learning models are able to identify more complex patterns that standard machine learning models are unable to recognize, simply because of the greater quantity of data used.

Deep learning is used in a variety of software, including those used for image recognition, product recommendation, and even for self-driving cars. Deep learning expands upon machine learning to produce highly advanced software systems, programs, and robotics.

Basic Fundamentals of Deep Learning

While deep learning is a more advanced approach to machine learning, the fundamentals are similar between the two. Each involves testing out a model and training it to perform specific tasks. The major difference is that deep learning machines can perform more challenging tasks, and often can be trained to perform more than one job. This is because of the neural networks that are created for the models. While machine learning networks are often easier and faster to train, deep learning networks, or architectures, have significantly more layers and algorithms.

Deep Learning Architecture

1. Generative

Generative models, or GAN, consist of a generator and a discriminator. These two deep learning models are trained simultaneously and compete against one another. One model focuses on generating new examples, while the other focuses on classifying the new examples generated by the first model. The success of this model depends on both the deep learning model's function and operation. If one fails to perform correctly, the whole system fails. Though each model depends on the other, they are both trained individually. This training process can take an extended amount of time.

2. Discriminative

Discriminative deep learning models are also known as conditional models. These models use statistical classifications to model or produce the optimal output by observing data. Discriminative models learn how to predict the conditional probability by learning the probability distribution of the data. The Bayes Theorem is utilized to assist the model in determining these probabilities. This theorem helps calculate the probability of one event based on how it connects to another event. The equation most commonly used for this theorem is written as:

$$P(A \mid B) = P(B \mid A)P(A) / P(B)$$

This type of model is favored in the medical field, as it can be trained to accurately find false positives and false negatives in testing done on patients.

3. Hybrid

Hybrid models utilize both generative and discriminative features. These models are used frequently when researchers want to train them to perform human action recognition. Hybrid models fuse together the homogeneous convolutional neural network classifiers, which ensure the input features are diverse by adjusting the initialization of the weights attached to the neural networks. This model is commonly used for feature recognition, voice recognition, and other human-based recognition patterns.

Creating a Deep Learning Model

Deep learning models are created either from scratch, transferred learning, or feature extraction. Each model is used to solve specific problems, and it is through your data that you will be able to best identify which is best suited to your data science project.

From Scratch

A deep learning model trained from scratch is used when there is a new application being tested. Typically, these types of models will result in a large amount of output produced. These are the least used models because of how long it can take to train the networks due to the substantial size of labeled data sets that need to be inputted. The architecture that is used will often need to learn the new model design as well as features; hence, the reason the learning rate takes much longer.

Transfer Learning

In a transfer learning model, a pre-trained model is used, the networks are already established, and new data is inputted. With this type of deep learning model, the networks are adjusted so a new task can be learned. The transfer learning model is the most commonly used type of model, as it does not require as much data to be learned and therefore, only takes a few minutes for new tasks to be processed.

Some pre-trained neural network models include AlexNet, GoogleNet, Xception, and Squeezenet.

Feature Extraction

The feature extraction model is a highly specialized deep learning model. It is the least common, as it utilizes the networks as feature extractors. Each layer is trained to learn a specific feature, and when necessary, these layers can then be pulled from the model and used as input for a machine learning model.

Each model is constructed using algorithms that allow the model to input, process, and understand large amounts of data. Some of the most common algorithms used with deep learning models include:

- Convolutional Neural Networks, or CNN
- Deep Boltzmann machine, or DBM
- Deep Belief Networks, or DBN
- Long-Short Term Memory Networks, or LSTMs
- Recurrent Neural Networks, or RNNS
- Stacked Auto-Encoders

How Does Deep Learning Relate to Data Science?

Deep learning relies on big data sets to train models. The data is what allows the program to function without the need for human intervention. Data science is used to determine which data sets are necessary to train the model to produce the most optimal results. Much in the same way that data science is used for traditional machine learning, it is used for deep learning. The only difference worth pointing out is the amount of data that is not only needed to be obtained to find a solution, but also the amount of data that needs to be collected in order to train the model properly.

Chapter 6
Deep Learning and
Neural Networks

"Much of what we do with machine learning happens beneath the surface. Machine learning drives our algorithms for demand forecasting, product search ranking, product and deals recommendations, merchandising placements, fraud detection, translations, and much more. Though less visible, much of the impact of machine learning will be of this type— quietly but meaningfully improving core operations."

-Jeffz Bezos

What are Neural Networks?

Neural networks are used in machine learning and deep learning, and resemble the neural networks of the human brain. Neural networks are the layers which algorithms pass through. The algorithm then goes through various processes and transformations that are both linear and nonlinear.

Standard neural networks are created with only a few hidden layers. Deep neural networks, on the other hand, can have hundreds of hidden layers, which is why they can perform human tasks with such accuracy.

Basic Neural Network Components:

Neural networks are composed of a number of features, though the nodes and layers are often the main focus. Most neural networks will feature the following list of components:

1. Neurons, or nodes, are the most basic units of a neural network. Each neuron in a network tends to have a specific function. They are responsible for receiving the input, triggering the activation function, and passing along that input to the next layer.

2. Weights are applied to the input connection between the nodes and are used by the neurons to determine what type of output it will produce and what activation function it needs to utilize. In every layer of the networks, the neurons weigh the inputs and then react accordingly to produce the most desired output.

3. Bias is added to hidden layers which can shift a learned function, so it overlaps with a previously learned function. They affect when the activation function is triggered without the need for input, so the appropriate output is produced.

4. Activation functions are responsible for determining what neurons need to be activated or what information needs to be passed to the next layer. If the activations are missing or not implemented correctly, the ability for the networks to learn will decrease significantly.

Common activation functions:

- Sigmoid, written as $f(x) = 1/1+ exp(-X)$, this activation function is used when the output is a predicted probability. When graphed, this will form an *S* curve.
- ReLU rectified linear units—if the input is greater than zero, the value returned is the input number, while if the input is less than zero, the value returned is zero.
- Softmax, used when there are multi-class classifications.

5. Neural network layers can vary in how many layers there are in each network, as well as how many neurons or nodes are found in each layer. In deep networks, there are multiple layers, each processing the data, learning from it and then passing what was learned on to the next

layer. That layer will then process whatever information was learned from the previous layer and expand on what can be learned before passing it along to the next layer. This continues until it reaches the output layer, where it will then be able to answer, make a prediction, or identify what the original data was. The number of layers allows for a deeper learning that occurs with the model.

When a neural network layer contains multiple nodes than a typical hidden layer would include, this is referred to as a wide network. A wider neural network does not result in being able to learn more from one layer to the next but does result in a higher number of concepts being learned.

6. Forward propagation is where a possibility of the question being asked is formulated. This is also referred to as the observed value.

7. Backpropagation, or the gradient descent, is where the error between the possible answer established with forward propagation and the actual correct answer to the question is reduced. This is also referred to as the expected value. With backpropagation, the gradient of the loss/error functions are calculated and then the parameters are adjusted to improve these results.

8. Cost function determines the difference between the forward propagation or observed value, and the backpropagation or expected value passes. This then determines the total error. Ultimately, the cost function will rate how well the network performs. The most common cost function used is the root mean square or quadratic cost.

9. The learning rate is a hyperparameter that has a positive value usually between .0 and 1.0. When neural networks are being trained, the weights are often updated to improve the output results. This rate indicates how quickly the network model is able to learn or solve a problem. How frequently the weights are updated reveals the learning rate.

10. Batches are types of hyperparameters used with gradient descent. The batch size refers to how many samples are used during a neural network's model training. Once it has gone through a specified number of samples, the internal parameters will be updated.

11. Epochs are types of hyperparameters used with gradient descent that determine how many passes through a data set the neural network must complete.

Most Common Neural Networks

1. Deep Feedforward Networks

Deep feedforward networks are also known as multilayer perceptrons or MLP. This is the most basic neural network. This neural network contains at least one input layer, a hidden layer, and an output layer. Each layer is connected to the next through the neurons or nodes. It is best used with structured data, and is the easiest to understand for beginners.

2. Convolution Network

Also referred to as CNN or ConvNet, the convolutional neural network is the most popular type of neural networks used in machine learning. This network is capable of inputting 2D data and does not need a manual feature extraction. This is beneficial as most forms of 2D data are images, and you would need to implement additional features that would allow the system to identify the data as such. Instead, the model is taught to identify the data automatically as an image by training it through collections of images. When the model is trained, each of its hidden layers—which can be in the hundreds—are programmed to detect varying features of the images. In one layer, it may be taught to identify what the edges of an image are; in another layer, it can be trained to identify shapes, colors, or objects. Each hidden layer detects more complex aspects of an image, which is why this type of network is mostly used for image recognition tasks.

There are four stages in CNN design:

1. *Convolution stage.* This is when the input signals are established.

2. *Subsampling stage.* During this stage, the input passed from the convolution layer and filters are adjusted to reduce their sensitivity to noise and other disturbances.

3. *Activation stage.* During the third stage, the layers are given control over how the input is passed from one layer to the next. This is similar to how the neurons of the brain operate.

4. *Fully connected stage.* During the final stage, all the layers form a connection so that each layer connects to the one before it.

What makes this type of network unique are the convolutional networks, as well as the pooling layers. Convolutional networks read the spatial patterns of the data inputted as opposed to every single feature of the data as a standalone piece. Filters are established to determine how spatial patterns are detected. The pooling layers follow the convolutional layers, and these obtain the important information needed to pass along to the next layers. Specific methods need to be programmed for this passing along of information, and the size of the layers needs to be determined based on the amount of data that is being inputted. This reduces the mathematical work required by the subsequent layers. The final segment of this network flattens the information into an extended neural network before being moved along to the fully connected multi-layer perceptron.

3. Recurrent Network

With recurrent neural networks or RNNs, the sequence of information is crucial for the overall success. These neural networks implement a type of memorization, where what has occurred in an earlier layer is remembered because there is a high probability that it will have an impact on the future layers and is often repeated. The networks all share parameters from one step to the next, and each requires a specific task to be performed. While these neural networks are useful for building chatbots and for natural language processing applications, they are not ideal for deep models because they cannot be stacked.

Neural Networks Algorithms

What distinguishes classical neural networks from deep learning neural networks is simply the amount of data that is inputted and how much the machine is able to handle. Classical neural networks tend to have fewer layers and, therefore, can be programmed, trained, and tested in a shorter amount of time. They also tend to perform more simplified and basic tasks. Deep learning neural networks are much more complex, requiring significantly more data and a longer trial and error period for testing and training.

The most common algorithms used with classical neural networks models include:

- Back-Propagation
- Hopfield Network
- Multilayer Perceptrons, or MLP
- Perception
- Radial Basis Function Networks, or RBFN
- Stochastic Gradient Descent

Why are Neural Networks Important for Deep Learning?

In deep learning, neural networks are the systems in which the machine is trained. Through progressive learning, these neural networks will be able to mimic human behavior through the use of algorithms and data. Without deep neural networks, a majority of the tasks expected from the machine would be impossible.

Neural networks are trained through an iterative learning process. Rows of data are fed into the machine model, one at a time. Weights are added and values are adjusted with each new row of data. The model is evaluated each time a row of data is fed through it. When we input some new data, the evaluations are also inputted. The machine then makes adjustments according to the evaluations and is able to make better choices with the latest information. This is how neural networks are trained to teach themselves.

While self-learning neural networks seem to be a scary and even taboo subject to discuss, there is a great misconception about how these machines learn. It is only through the evaluation and human adjustment that a machine is capable of learning, even with deep learning neural networks. While machines can perform human-like recognition, that is simply because that is what they have been programmed to do. A machine, at this time, is unable to learn new information without first being trained to recognize or perform these new tasks.

Chapter 7
The Parameters and Hyper Parameters of Deep Learning

"If you've found something that works, should you just keep doing it? Or is it better to try new things, knowing it could be a waste of time but also might lead to a better solution? Would you rather be a cowboy or a farmer? Start a company or run an existing one? Go steady or play the field? A midlife crisis is the yearning to explore after many years spent exploiting."

-Pedro Domingos

What are the Deep Learning Parameters?

Deep learning parameters, or trained parameters, are learned through the training process. Parameters are not exclusive to deep learning methods; they are also utilized in various simple machine learning models, as well. In the deep learning method, there will be a much higher number of parameters and you will need to have a deeper understanding of how each one can affect the output.

These parameters are calculated by counting the parameters in the layers and then obtaining the sum of all the parameters in the whole network, which is done through some simple arithmetic.

Inputs X outputs = weights

The number of outputs is equal to the number of nodes of that layer.

The weights equal the number of parameters of that layer.

If a bias was also added to the layer, you would add these to the weight. Note that the number of biases you have for each layer should equal the number of nodes in that layer.

Input X outputs + bias = weights

You would do this calculation for each layer and then add up all the weights from each one to get the total number of learnable parameters in that network.

Convolutional Neural Network Parameters

In convolutional networks, you must also take into consideration the filters added to the layers, as well. These filters may be referred to as kernels. To calculate the parameters in these networks, you not only need to count the number of filters, but also consider the size of these filters. Not all layers of a convolutional network will be convolutional or have these filters but can be a typical network layer or dense layer. This is where calculating the parameters for these types of networks can become confusing. Before outputting data from a dense layer, it also needs to be flattened, which results in some additional calculations.

If the previous layer was dense, then your input would be the number of nodes in that layer. Your output would be the number of filters multiplied by the size of the filter, and the bias would equal the number of filters. For example, if you have an input layer that contains three nodes followed by a hidden layer that contains two filters, each filter size is 2 X 2 and have bias added. Your equation for that hidden layer would go:

Input = 3

output = 2 X 2 = 4 X 2 = 8

learned parameters = 3 x 8 = 24 weights + 2 = 26 learn parameters

If, however, the layer prior was a convolutional layer, then the only thing that changes is the input would equal the number of filters from the previous layer instead of the number of nodes.

Now, if you are going from a convolutional layer to a dense output layer, you will need to flatten the layer. Here, you would not take the inputs from the previous convolutional layer—instead, you would need to use the dimension from the size of data that was originally inputted in the first computing layer. You would multiply the dimension of the data size and then multiply that number by the number of filters in the previous layer. For example, your original data was 10 X 10. The layer prior to your output layer contains 3 filters. Your output layer contains 2 nodes and there is bias added to the output layer. Your equation would go:

Input = 10 X 10 = 100 X 3 = 300

Output = 2

Learned parameters = 300 X 2 = 600 + 2= 602 learned parameters

You would calculate the total parameters for each individual network by adding up all the parameters from each layer.

What are Deep Learning Hyper-Parameters?

Where parameters are established through the training process, hyper-parameters are established before training begins. The learning rate and the layers of the network are considered hyperparameters, and these need to be set before any algorithms are assigned to a model.

Hyperparameters fall into one of two categories: optimizer hyperparameters or machine-specific hyperparameters. The learning rate, batch size, and the number of epochs are all types of hyperparameters. These hyperparameters affect either the training process or have an effect on the structure of the model being used.

Learning Rate

Learning rates are hyperparameters that need to be carefully considered so that optimal results are achieved. A small learning rate results in a neural network being trained for an extensive amount of time and still being unable to reach optimal results. If the learning rate is set too high, then the network makes predictions too soon where optimal results are missed.

Batch Size

Batch training refers to the process of entering all the data into the training step. Then, all the examples of data sets are reviewed in order to determine the margin of error. The batch size will have a direct effect on the training process and the time this step will take.

While large batch sizes can help give a computational boost to the training size, significantly more memory is needed. On the other hand, smaller batch sizes add noise to error calculations. This can actually reduce the risk of the process being stopped at a minima. Typically, an ideal batch size should fall around 32.

Epoch

An epoch is when an entered data set has been passed through the neural network forward and backward. Each data set is typically broken up into batches, and each batch equals an itinerary. When all itineraries have been run through the network, an epoch is completed. Epochs tend to be a high number, as they are set based on the validation error. You want to have a high number of epochs to minimize the error of the machine.

How to Optimize Learning Parameters?

Setting the appropriate hyperparameters is a vital step in deep learning and machine learning. These fundamental elements need to be carefully selected for optimal performance. Parameters can be selected either manually or automatically. Selecting hyperparameters manually will require a clear and in-depth understanding of the model being used, and can impact computational costs. Additionally, when using a deep learning model as opposed to a simpler machine learning model, the automatic hyperparameters are often not able to consider the full aspects of deep learning scenarios.

Hyperparameter tuning can be a very long process and tends to have four distinct parts.

1. The objective function is the part that scores how well the hyperparameters perform based on the values you want to minimize or maximize.
2. The domain refers to the hyperparameters being searched for.
3. The algorithm is the method in which hyperparameters are selected and how the objection function scores the performance.
4. The result history is the data produced from the hyperparameter sets and includes the objective function scoring.

There are four common ways data scientists optimize parameters. The first is a trial-and-error process, where hyperparameters are simply tested at random with no logical approach. While this approach can be great if you are just learning about setting hyperparameters, as you will gain a better understanding of data science teams, this is not the ideal solution for setting hyperparameters. Most data science projects will use either grid search, random search, or Bayesian optimization methods.

Grid Search

The grid search approach to hyperparameter optimization builds a model for every possible hyperparameter option. You begin by creating a grid that shows each potential hyperparameter combination. Then, each combination is used in its own test model, and each model is evaluated to test its accuracy. After all the models have been tested and evaluated, you would then use the set of parameters that performed the best in your actual model. While this can yield favorable results, it is a time-consuming process and requires a great deal more resources than most data science projects allow for.

Random Search

Random searches may look a lot like the grid search approach, but can be less time consuming and much more effective. With random search optimization, you set up your grid and then randomly select a combination to test out. This can result in finding a baseline much faster, and the randomization depends on how much time and resources you have. When you randomly select hyperparameters, you can easily see which parameters are performing closest to your expected results and then you can fine-tune the parameters further by making slight adjustments.

Bayesian Optimization

With this approach to hyperparameter optimization, you create a test model to evaluate how effective different sets of hyperparameters are. This can be one of the most effective ways to decide on which hyperparameters will work optimally with your actual model. The only downside is the process where you can typically only work with numerical parameters. This also tests out only one variable at a time, which can make the processing time-consuming.

Cross-Validation

What makes the optimization process take a great deal of time has much to do with the cross-validation. Cross-validation is needed because the data used when testing parameters cannot be the same data used when training your actual model. Testing data can only be used once, and if used when testing parameters, you will optimize the parameters based on this data—therefore, when the model is tested it will not yield the most accurate results. Instead, a validation set of data is needed to test the hyperparameters. Cross-validation sets are created to better test the performance of each hyperparameter set without corrupting the valuable training data. These cross-validation sets are tested multiple times to assess for optimal performance and to reduce the risk of overfitting.

Early Stopping

What happens if, halfway through the training or optimization process, your model is performing terribly or is doing the opposite of what you expect it to do? When you begin your training and optimization process, most often, you need to simply wait until the model is done with the computation phase. This can be a huge waste of valuable time. Some frameworks allow you to set up early stopping guidelines before the training begins. With this feature, you can set expectations for converging rates, how the model performs compared to the baseline, and if the model is stalling out. If the model fails to reach certain expectations during the training process, it will automatically stop. You can also set up time limits, where the training will stop after a specific amount of time. This results in using your resources more efficiently and reduces the wasting of time and focus.

Chapter 8
Presenting Data

"Data are just summaries of thousands of stories—tell a few of those stories to help make the data meaningful."

-Chip Heath and Dan Heath

Why does Data Presentation Matter?

In data science, being able to interpret and communicate models used and your resulting data is crucial. The most important aspect of the presentation lies in the actionable insight. It is this insight that will teach others how to repeat the desired outcome and how to avoid any negative consequences.

Data Reporting

Reporting your data is the way the findings from all your efforts becomes known. This data report will often be passed along to industry professionals, and they will be tested even further by other data science teams. For this reason, these reports should be carefully crafted and adhere to industry standards. The amount of detail you reveal in these reports is essential for building your credibility. While this, in the data science process, can be overwhelming and stressful, it is actually quite a simple process.

1. *Have a clear understanding of the audience who will be receiving the reports.* As with any writing, your audience is the main focus. Your report should be written with clear, understandable language that your readers can relate to. An effective way to ensure that you are writing with your audience in mind is to

consider the audience as those who you have collaborated with, the executives of the company, and the technical staff. When you keep in mind all these different types of individuals, you will be able to get your main points across in a more concise way that motivates your readers to make use of the information themselves.

2. *Go over all your results multiple times.* You want to ensure that the report you write is an accurate representation of your findings. Before writing your report, examine all the information you have once again and reanalyze the data you will be including.

3. *Once you are confident with your data analysis, properly organize and create visuals that represent the data.* You want to create an in-depth spreadsheet of all the data you used throughout the process. Even if your final report and analysis do not include some of the data, you still want it to be a part of your spreadsheet. Once you have successfully created your spread, you should look over it and determine how your data can be transformed into a visual. Highly relevant and pertinent data should be made into a chart, graph, or other visual, which will allow your audience to easily understand and see the results.

Structuring Your Data Report

When it comes time to sit and write out your report, you want to follow a basic outline. Keeping it simple is the best approach, and the following outline gives you a clear idea of how to accomplish this.

Introduction

The first part of your report will open with the introduction. Here, you will give a brief summary of the full report. You will also want to give attention to the data and subject matter. The introduction is where you want to state why you conducted the study and explain your analysis question or the question your project focused on answering.

Your intro should end with a conclusion that will give your audience a short overview of what is included in the report.

Body

The body of your report should be divided into four distinct parts.

- **Data.** In this section, you will refer to your spreadsheet so you can clearly describe the data you used.
- **Method.** In the method section, you will explain how you gathered your data and how it was processed. You also want to go over how you analyzed the data.
- **Analysis.** The analysis section is where you want to include any visuals you created to represent your data. Here, you should give an in-depth explanation of how you conducted your analysis.
- **Results.** In the final section of the body, you will go over what you found. You want to clearly explain the results that were produced through the analysis you conducted.

Conclusion

Your data report conclusion should restate the question you presented in the introduction of your report. You will also highlight the most important results from the analysis, then end your conclusion with additional recommendations for further analysis or testing and what data should be included.

Appendix

At the very end of your report, you should include an appendix area. This area is dedicated to all the details of the process you embarked on. You will also want to add secondary data that provides additional information and any references.

How to Properly Use Visuals to Present Data

Visualization used in presenting your data needs to be useful and understandable. As mentioned earlier, visuals are key to driving your facts home in an eye-catching and memorable way. Data visualization uses various charts, slides, graphics, and text to better explain patterns and trends in the data collected. This allows data scientists to communicate the importance and relevance of the data used. Your visuals should be clear, use appropriate text and colors, and relate to what you are saying at the time.

Some things to keep in mind when creating visuals:

1. Visuals should help tell your story.
2. Using icons can be an easy way to bring the audience's attention to specific facts.
3. Instead of using bullets to separate your ideas, use icons that will keep your presentation more interesting.
4. Using a bold font will make the words jump out to the audience—be sure to use this for vital information and statistics.
5. Use a variety of visuals that can engage your audience more.
6. Choose your colors wisely. You want your icons, text, and charts to stand out from the background. Using a darker background with light text and icon colors can make these elements pop in your presentation.
7. Be careful of the colors you used for charts and graphs—you do not want these to blend with the background.
8. Think about the mood or tone you want to set for the presentation and use colors that will complement that.

How to use Storytelling to Support Your Data

Storytelling is a key skill that can strengthen the importance of your message. Up until now, data science has predominantly involved the use of technical skills. When you are presenting your data to an audience of individuals who have little to no technical background, having only those technical skills will make it difficult for you to translate the information in a way that triggers an action. Unless you are able to effectively tell a clear story based on the data collected, all your technical skills will have gone to waste. Your story should provide your audience with easy-to-follow steps and a deeply rooted "why" for them to begin taking those steps. You want your report to build through the course of your presentation and guide your audience from one step to the next. Below is a simple outline that can help you effectively create a storyline within your presentation.

1. Set the scene.

Setting the scene is the most crucial step in your storytelling. If you are unable to capture the audience's attention from the beginning, you will have very few people listening along the way. This is done in the introduction of your presentation. The scene you set should focus around the problem your research is trying to solve, the urgency to solve that problem, why it is important for you, and interesting aspects about the problems that will grab the audience's attention. You want to be sure the audience has a clear understanding of why you conducted the research and the impact it can have on them. When you set the scene, you want your audience to be able to instantly relate to what you are saying. When you are able to do this, it will be difficult for the audience not to continue to listen to what you have to say.

2. The hypothesis or solution for the settings.

Once you have properly set up your scene, you want to transition into the hypothesis or the solution you want your audience to focus on. During this part of your storytelling, you want to make it clear to your audience why your hypothesis is the answer to the problem you presented in your introduction or your scene-setting. You should use this opportunity to entice the audience further to learn more, and you will be able to transition them into the first step of your method easily.

3. Methodology

When you are walking the audience through your methods and process, you want the information to be concise and to the point. You don't want to go over every single long, drawn-out equation utilized, but you do want to highlight the key steps you took that helped you prove or disprove your hypothesis. Be humble—you do not need to show off every single skill set you used along the way. Instead, use visuals during this part of your storytelling to highlight the most important aspects of the approach you took. You want to give enough information about the work you conducted to give your audience a clear idea of what you did and why, but also leave enough out so that those who are interested in learning more about the specific details and technical approaches will follow up.

4. Related work

It is essential to point out how the method and approach you took with your research is different from what has been done before. This part of your storyline should intrigue the audience further, but it can be difficult to maintain your audience's attention through this section. What is important to do with this step is to show how your solution, method, and work stands out from other techniques and ideas that already exist. How is what you did any different than what has already been done a hundred times? It is important to draw reference to work that has been done before but do so in a way that allows you to expand and improve upon those methods and ideas.

5. Results

The next step is to show your results or the contributions your research made. Your results should highlight the problem you have solved, the knowledge or deeper understanding you bring to a specific industry or field, and strengthen your overall storyline.

6. Outlook

While your work may have produced some spectacular results and made groundbreaking contributions, there are bound to be some limitations you haven't addressed yet. Every research project has its own set of limits, and when the limits do not retrain the work you are able to do, you will be able to yield even grander results. You want to take the time to point out the limitations you encounter through your work and address how you can remove this limitation in future work. This will close your storyline, so you want to end with a powerful conclusion that emphasizes the future impact this research can have.

Creating a Presentation

Your visuals and the storyline of your data science reports are the two driving forces that will turn your written reports into an unforgettable presentation. Aside from these two aspects, there are some additional elements that you want to give attention to.

1. Structure

You want to invite the audience to experience the process of how and why your research was conducted. The introduction of your presentation is what can ultimately set the stage for the rest of your speech. If your opening section is bland, unclear, or rushed through, you will miss out on a vital opportunity to capture the audience's attention. You want the introduction to give enough information about yourself, the reason for your research or the problem you tried to solve, and provide them with just enough information about the process that makes them eager to learn more. You want to walk the audience step by step through the research, and along with each step, you will build upon your storyline. Each step should give the audience a clear goal or obstacle that needed to be reached or overcome. This is how you will create a compelling storyline that is engaging, entertaining, and even inspiring.

2. Slides

Professional slides can influence the quality of your presentation. Slides that are visually appealing, informative, and are well-thought-out to accompany your speech will keep your audience's attention. Effective slides are ones that provide just enough information so the audience can gain a general understanding of what you are talking about at the moment. You don't want to distract your audience by putting too much on your slides, as they will tend to zone out on what you are saying to understand what they are reading. Keep slides clutter-free and think of them as visual aids that give your words a boost of excitement.

3. The contributions

The main focus of your data reports will be about your results. Put more emphasis on the technical contributions of the work, as this is the greatest impact it will have. How will the research you conducted impact industries, businesses, or increase the general knowledge or awareness around the subject matter? The contributions made are a key piece to your storyline, and this should be clearly delivered through your presentation.

4. Entertaining

How you deliver your presentation will have a direct impact on the value of the information you present. You want to ensure that the language you use is clear and correct. Your presentation should flow smoothly from one point to the next, without hesitation. You want to keep your audience engaged in what you are staying, which is where a few appropriate and entertaining lines can go a long way. Your data science report is filled with valuable information, but a little humor can enhance your presentation and make it more relatable for your audience.

5. Confidence

It is not easy for everyone to speak publicly, as it is one of the top phobias around the world, but you need to have confidence in the way you address your audience. If you have put the time into practicing the way you will deliver your presentation, you can increase your confidence going into it. If you have given yourself adequate time to prepare, practice, and know that you have done all the work you can, you will automatically feel more at ease when it comes time to address your audience.

Conclusion

Data is easily accessible, but without any use for it, all it is is just a collection of numbers and characters. Data science takes this data, turns it into information, and gives it purpose. Whether you began this book assuming that data science was a complex term or was too simple a term, you now have a deeper understanding of what it is as a whole. Data science is a process, and this process is used to find solutions for a number of pressing concerns for businesses and industries.

Throughout this book, it has been highlighted how data science and big data are interconnected and how they are simultaneously used for technology solutions. Without data science, machine learning and deep learning may not be possible—or, at the very least, would not have advanced as rapidly has it has in recent years.

This book has offered you a starting point to become more knowledgeable in a number of areas that data science impacts. You have learned how data science affects many aspects of machine learning, how it ensures the most relevant and valuable data is used with deep learning, and how it can be used to help set parameters in neural networks. You may be wondering just what data science can influence. It has been the goal throughout these pages for you to gain a clear understanding of some complex methods, ideas, and practices.

As it is now, data science has great potential to be a world-changing approach to not just how businesses operate, but how people communicate with one another, how countries are governed, the environment, the medical field—it seems as if there is not a thing on this planet that may not be directly or indirectly affected by the growth of data science.

Hopefully, this book has inspired you to learn more about data, data science, and deep learning. Maybe it has inspired you to learn more about programming or coding. Maybe you have a desire to seek out data on your own to answer some burning questions you might have. As you should have gathered by now, there are not many places where data science would not provide some benefit. How will it benefit you?

Bonus Material
Book Title: Building a Massive Social Following
Build your Brand's Following using Leading Strategies and Tips

Social media is intensely categorized by its connectivity, interactivity, and of course, user-driven dialogue and content. Thankfully in today's world, social media usage has become a necessity of daily life. The majority of people make use of social media, and its associated networks to access information and news. Social networks can also be used to interact socially and help influence decision making on a vast array of issues and topics.

Social networks have become a very respected tool for communication enabling users to talk to others all over the world. It also allows users to create, spread, and share information. Brands are now able to make use of social networks to influence customer purchases via advertising, marketing, and reviews. At their core, social networks have vastly transformed the way we communicate, the way we create and develop bonds, the way we access and share information.

Understanding Social Networks

When the term social network is mentioned, social networking platforms come to mind. Sites such as Twitter, Facebook, Blogger, LinkedIn, and Tumblr are household names, regardless of how many active users they have. It would not be wrong to presume that almost everyone around the world has heard of Facebook and every individual aged between 14-50 has at one point or another had a Facebook account. Considering that social networks have the ability to make the world a smaller but much-connected community.

This translates to people being able to connect with old friends and loved ones. Businesses can conduct meetings with participants being on the other side of the world. There are just so many possibilities to communication that have been fueled by social networks. Social networks at their inception were mainly for personal use, enabling people to connect with those in their community and organize events in a much more coordinated way, but there is another aspect to social networks that has grown exponentially over the years. Businesses have been making use of social media during candidate interviews, as a sort of background check on individuals, they are looking to hire.

Some businesses have chosen to take it a step further by conducting interviews via social media networks like Facebook or Google Hangouts. Teams can come together during virtual meetings to brainstorm and come up with solutions that would otherwise have to be rescheduled until all participants were in the same locale. This ease of communication has eradicated a few of the logistical issues associated with meetings and team projects. It can definitely be said that the society we know and love today has become extraordinarily intertwined and dependent on social networks. Social networks have taken over our lives as our primary communication and connectivity tool.

Social networks, as stated earlier, has had an effect on nearly every area of our lives but none so much as the effect it has had on journalism and news. Considering that the internet is the quickest and most seamless way to get the latest information and news, traditional media houses have had to resort to placing their content online. Information that was initially available via print media has become widely available online via social networks. People can discover the events taking place and shaping their world. They are also able to discuss these events amongst themselves, fostering dialogue and interconnectivity. Social networks have also enabled and given power to the average individual to break stories happening around them.

Social networking sites, such as Twitter and Facebook have seen an increase in amateur journalism; people can produce and share the news that they believe is credible and accurate. Social networks in the eyes of the masses mean instant information and that is reaffirmed by the fact that we can nearly instantly share, create, and publish stories of any kind ranging from gossip to news about natural disasters. There is now a lot more news being broken on social networking sites such as Facebook and Twitter more than traditional mediums.

The influence that social networks have on our lives cannot be understated, as the way we think, the way we react, the decisions we make are now being influenced by what we see and what other people share on social networking sites. For instance, we can make somewhat informed decisions about restaurants, companies, colleges, products, and more by merely paying attention to blogs and reviews posted online. Our decisions are formed and influenced by the choices that other people make.

Social networks, as stated earlier, have an integral role in the way life has been shaped today. The tools that comprise of social networks are web-based, and they have enabled and actively fueled discovery, knowledge acquisition, the sharing of philosophies and ideas. We are now able to interact with more and more people every day, and organizations can connect with more of their target audience. Social networks have completely transformed the way we live, making communication much more manageable and accessible. User-generated content has become the norm with pictures, data, and videos made by the average person gaining ground and visibility.

Additionally, social networks have opened up another frontier for brands and individuals alike looking to gain an advantage in the world of marketing. This has been categorized by an immense upsurge of brands and companies that engage in internet and digital marketing. It can be safe to say that almost every company has a presence on at least one social networking site and those with no presence are at the risk of being left behind. Digital marketing has become so interconnected with social networks that social network marketing has become the standard bearer for online marketing campaigns. It is safe to bet that social networking is going to have a massive influence on whatever is to come in the marketing sphere. The sky appears to be the starting point for how social networks can influence and affect the way brands market themselves and their goods.

The Possibilities of Social Networks

The possibilities are seemingly endless for social media. It is uncommon for people to go a day without using or referring to social media. Whether it is used for communicating, learning, or decision making, social media is here to stay and will continue to affect our society. There have been numerous studies carried out to show that a large percentile of the population spends at least a quarter of their time online on social networks. This amount of time shows how ingrained social networks have become in our lives.

There are numerous facets to social media with fields like welfare, food, entertainment, business, and more benefiting from the advantages that social media has to offer. It is an essential tool for not just businesses but entrepreneurs looking to maximize the visibility of their brand. Social networks help bridge the gap between customers and brands as the brands can quickly and seamlessly deliver valuable information to their target audience.

Below are a few reasons why social networks are essential:

- In today's world, it is the norm for businesses to have a specialized team to handle their social network outreach, so much so that more than 80% of businesses include social networks in their marketing strategy.

- Businesses with a social network focused marketing campaign have noticed an increase in sales value over three years.
- A little more than 50% of individual marketers have taken a complete workday to develop and maintain their social network marketing strategies.

There are a few reasons why it makes perfect sense for an individual and a brand to have a social network presence:

Communication

Social networking sites, such as Twitter and Facebook, have broken down much of the barriers to communication that have plagued humanity. It is so easy in today's world to go to Facebook, search for a long lost love or a former classmate online, and send a message. This has been further helped by the advent of smartphones, placing the resources and power that were initially found only in a personal computer or laptop in the palm of our hands, regardless of where we are in the world.

Media Sharing

Thanks to Instagram, Snapchat, and Facebook, we are now able to share pictures of the most memorable parts of our lives with family and friends, regardless of their location in the world. Family members who had to wait until a special occasion brought them together can now share in the loving moments of others with just a click.

Heightened Awareness for Social Issues

This is one of the most glaring aspects of human life that social media has transformed. Many make use of numerous social networks to raise awareness and money for different charities and causes. The most famous of them was the ice bucket challenge awareness campaign for ALS in 2014.

This campaign was one that was created organically, which means it started as a few people looking to bring awareness to a cause of theirs and users on social networks picked it up and ran with it, making it go viral. There have also been numerous GoFundMe campaigns in which people that have gone through a tough time can depend on the kindness of strangers to give towards whatever goal they have in mind.

Promotions

Entrepreneurs and brands have made use of social networks to promote just about anything. Corporations in the world of entertainment and business, as well as people, can promote their goods, services, and work, while also increasing their customer and follower base simply by publishing content and information concerning their work and any forthcoming events. This has made social networks transform from a communication tool to a sales tool.

Understanding Social Network Personalities

There is a school of thought that says there are two types of individuals on social networks. There are the meformers, and then there are the informers. Research carried out by Rutgers University showed that only around 20% of the active users on social networks are informers, with the rest being meformers. Before we explain how this is the key to gaining more followers, we first have to discuss what a 'meformer' and an 'informer' are.

Meformers can be described as individuals on social networks that post updates that mostly pertain to themselves. Informers are individuals on social networks that post content for information sharing purposes. This meformer terminology was actually coined by the research team at Rutgers after having analyzed data from a sample set of social networking accounts. The research team also looked to analyze usage patterns, as well as follower numbers and number of tweets. They discovered that there was a significant divide amongst those that shared self-related information and those that shared information on other topics themselves. This information was extremely vital as it showed that informers tended to have twice the number of followers as meformers did. This was a revelation, as it showed that the key to gaining followers on social networks was not to be self-oriented, but to focus more on providing information that can better those around you on social networks.

Determining Which You Are

Now if you are wondering how to ascertain if you are a meformer or an informer, you will have to pay attention to your posts on social media and the topic they contain. If it appears that a large portion of your posts tend to be about you or things related to you, then you are a meformer, however, if you are the type of individual that likes posting content that you deem could be helpful to others, or you like informing people on the current happenings in the world around them, then it is likely that you are an informer.

If you are a meformer, all is not lost, as it is possible for you to transform your social network identity into one that can be categorized as an informer. You have to attempt to increase how much information you share on your chosen social networks. Doing so helps those around you identify you as an informer rather than an informer. That being said, you should be careful to not overwhelm your current followers with too much information that they begin to feel like you are spamming them.

You should aim to be an authority figure in whatever subject matter or niche you select. Being a leader and a creator can help set you apart from the millions of other people looking to harness their chosen social network and build a massive social media following. When you attempt to make this transition from a meformer into an informer, it is crucial that you make it as smooth as possible. You can be at the risk of losing your followers, putting you back to square one if you do the following:

- Post too much in a very short timespan.
- Post content about topics that do not interest followers.
- Posting too much about the boring aspects of your life. Everyone has those boring moments, and they do not want to hear about yours.

Check out our Other *AMAZING* Titles:

1. Data Mining

A Handbook to Understanding Hidden Patterns in Data

A data mining system is a system designed and developed to mine data from various data sources. The number of data mining systems available today is huge. Data mining system combine technologies available from the following areas:

- Information retrieval.
- Image analysis.
- Pattern recognition.
- Signal processing.
- Spatial data analysis.
- Computer graphics.
- Business.
- Web technology.
- Bioinformatics.

Classification of Data Mining Systems

The following criterion helps classify a data mining system:

- Statistics.
- Information science.
- Database technology.
- Machine learning.

- Visualization.
- Information science.
- Other disciplines.

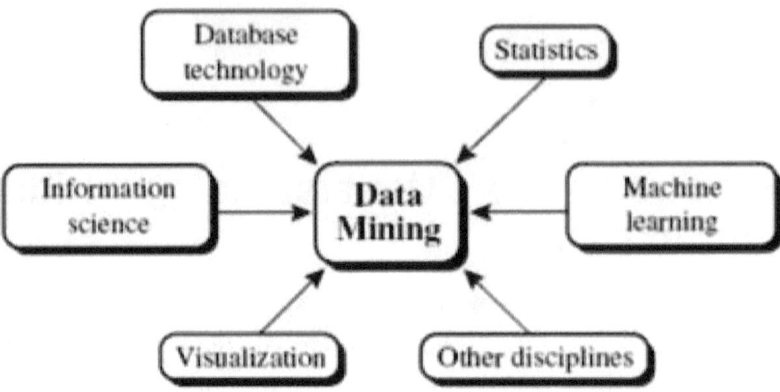

There are other aspects which help classify a data mining system. They are:

- The type of database.
- The type of knowledge.
- The type of techniques.
- The applications used and adapted.

Let us go through these classification methods one by one.

The Type of Database to Be Mined

If we consider the types of databases, we can get a better understanding of systems in data mining processes. There are various types of data, namely data types, data models, etc., that classify a system.

If a database is classified based on data models, the result would be an object-oriented, relational, transactional, or a data warehousing server.

The Type of Knowledge to Be Mined

Data mining systems are segregated based on the knowledge it can mine. The following functionalities will be taken into consideration for this classification.

- Discrimination.
- Characterization.
- Classification.
- Outlier analysis.
- Prediction.
- Correlation and association analysis.
- Evolution analysis.

The Type of Techniques Utilized

The mining techniques classify the system as well. The level of user interaction with the system helps to define the techniques used. The techniques are:

- Autonomous systems.
- Query-driven systems.
- Interactive-exploratory systems.

Alternatively, analysis methods used can help classify data too, the methods are:

- Machine learning.
- Visualization.
- Statistics.
- Data warehouse or database oriented.
- Neural networks.
- Pattern recognition.

A sophisticated and ideal data mining system will integrate various techniques. This ensures that the merits of individual techniques are available in one single system.

The Applications Used and Adapted

The applications that use the data mining systems can help classify the system as well. It is not necessary that a data mining system that works for one application may work as efficiently for another application as well. Different applications demand application-specific methods. Hence, a generic system won't work in some application-specific tasks. The applications are:

- Sales.
- Finance.
- DNA.
- Email.
- Telecommunications.
- Stock markets.

Integrating Data Mining Systems

The data mining output needs to be directed to another system. If this system does not have a place to store its output, such as a data warehouse or database, there is no goal set for the data mining activity. Therefore, there are data integration schemes created so that a data mining system communicates and feeds the output to a database or data warehouse.

Here is a look at some of the integration schemes:

No Coupling

In this system, a database or a data warehouse system does not communicate with each other. Functions of the data warehouse system don't get utilized by data mining procedures. The mining system then extracts data from all active data sources and stores it in a different file.

Loose Coupling

In this system, a database or data warehouse system may utilize some functions of the mining system. Data is collected from a data warehouse or database and it undergoes the mining process. The output gets stored in the database, the data warehouse, or a file.

Semi-tight coupling

In this system, functions of a database or a data warehouse system may be utilized by the data mining system. Additionally, the database will also contain implementations of some data mining techniques.

Tight Coupling

In this system, functions of a database or a data warehouse system may be applied smoothly to the mining system. The subsystem is considered together as one after mining.

Want to read more? Check our book 'Data Mining; A Handbook to Understanding Hidden Patterns in Data' on Amazon today!

2. Content Marketing:

Growth Strategies to Stay Ahead in the Changing World of Content Marketing and Maximize ROI

When it comes to content marketing, clients want proven results. They don't want to hire someone who may have simply written a few articles in the past and then hopefully will be able to put together a whole campaign to sell a product. They want someone who has experience, someone who has done this work before, can prove that the work was successful, and show that these clients are willing to pay a premium to get this.

Most clients understand that they are going to get what they pay for. If they are going to spend money on this campaign, and they want to make money on their product, they understand that they need to pick out a copywriter who knows what they are doing and can bring in results. The client would rather pay a little bit more to get the good results the first time rather than paying someone new to do the work, wasting time and money, and then having to pay the professional to come in and clean up the mess.

You will find that good clients know how much you are worth. If you are working with a client that wants to pay a low rate, there are a few things that are going on here. First, the client is either not aware of the current rate for a good copywriter and is just guessing at how much they will need to pay for the work to get done. Another issue could be that they are having issues with their cash flow and they are hoping for a miracle to happen, such as a good content marketing offering to do the services for a great price so they can get their business back up and running. And in other cases, the client is just trying to get work for free - they don't really care how hard you work, as long as they get the results that they want for a way below market value amount.

No matter the reason for the lower amount offered on a job, you don't want to work with any of these clients. The first client doesn't know your true value and may be difficult to work within the long term. Now you can talk to them about the price and some will realize that they need to pay more and will be happy to do it, but others will still want to get the discounted price because that is all they want to pay and they think the work is "easy enough for anyone to do." You don't want to work for these people because they won't value your work and you will spend way too much time making very little money.

For the second group of clients, you need to be careful. There is usually a reason that they are short on cash or have cash flow issues, and often this means that they are about to fail. You are not only going to miss out on some of the good income that you should be making, but the company is likely going to fail and you won't make a good income at all from them.

And finally, no one wants to work with someone who purposely puts the value too low. Many times, these clients disappear and never even pay, leaving you with a lot of wasted time and no money to show for it. Even if the client does end up paying you for the work that you do, you will find that they are really difficult to work with, will request way too many changes, and you will spend more time than it is worth to get the work done.

Finding the clients who will pay the rates that you deserve is critical. This is going to help out in a number of ways. First, they are going to value your time. Perhaps these clients have worked with some bad copywriters in the past and they are willing to pay more to get the results that they want, or they know the market value for what they want. Once you prove that you are the person they want to work with, you are going to be able to get those well-paying jobs that are going to make your income go through the roof.

But before you can work for these better prices, you need to make sure that you are able to produce those results. There are plenty of clients that will pay attractive rates but are not going to pay those rates to just anyone. You will need to have a method to show how you have been successful with these kinds of campaigns in the past. You will need to show some of the work that you have done with content marketing in the past, and if you have some numbers in place to show how successful they were, you will be able to impress the clients even more.

As a good copywriter, you should be able to show that you are going to bring in results for the client. A good client is willing to pay some of the higher rates, but you do need to make it worth their time. These clients are going to pay for the results, not just for your time to create the work. If there aren't any results, you are going to have some issues getting the income that you want.

The Power of Landing Pages

In the digital marketing and online business community, landing pages are crucial. They're the difference between a successful campaign and one that makes you question the results people claim to be getting.

The wrong ones will make the internet spew hate and vitriol then push you into a downward spiral leading to a long, slow, agonizing death.

The right landing pages turn browsers to fans, haters to friends, and customers to advocates. People share them on social media and the world creates hashtags in your honor.

There's a fine line between high performing landing pages and the ones that'll make you wonder if the time you spent on them was worth it.

Old advice like "use red in your headlines" and "create multiple columns on your pages" will kill conversions faster than a prize-winning thanksgiving turkey gets slaughtered.

Your audience is jaded.

They've been on the web for years. Many of them were born into the web and may know more about it than you.

You're doing yourself, your brand, and your customers a disservice by trying to get away with poorly designed and researched landing pages.

Why?

Because I know how powerful they are when used correctly. It's even more pronounced when you don't have much traffic. If your website is receiving a million visitors a month, you can disregard this book because you'll get customers and subscribers no matter what you do.

If you're like the rest of us mortals, then keep reading. You'll find gems in this book and learn how to create more powerful landing pages that move your business forward.

Before we dive into making the ultimate landing pages, you and I need to be on the same page.

A visitor can "land" on any page.

While those pages can and should be optimized for conversions (especially the about page, as it is one of the top three visited pages on a website), they're not what I'm referring to when I say landing page.

Whenever you see "landing pages" in this book, it refers to dedicated pages made and optimized to do one thing:

That could be to make a sale.

That could be to promote a sign up for a mailing list.

It could also be to promote a giveaway.

Whatever.

The overarching theme with the landing pages I discuss is they have one desired outcome. The rest of the pages on your website have too many distractions. Those include links in the body text, menu buttons, popups, footer links, a sidebar, etc.

Let's redefine landing pages to reflect the focus of this book.

Landing pages are standalone web pages distinct from your main website that has been designed for a single focused objective. This means your landing page shouldn't have global navigation, in-text links, or extraneous elements like a sidebar.

There are many types of landing pages.

1. Click through pages. These are pages, generally on e-commerce websites, used to promote clicking through to the next page where the sale can be made. Think of them as teaser pages which warm up the prospect for the main offer.

2. Lead generating pages. This is the most common type of landing page. Their focus is to get your visitor to part with their contact information so you can market to them later in a more controlled setting EG Email.

It's done by giving away something of value in exchange for the contact information. A few examples of lead magnets are:

- E-books

- Webinars

- Cheat sheets

- Video tutorials

- First chapter of a book

- Free consultations

- Contests

- Free trial

- Notifications on updates

- Whitepaper

3. Sales pages. The most important pages on your website. This is where the money is made and, by nature, has the lowest conversion rate. On average, e-commerce sites see a 2%-4% conversion rate, and SaaS companies see 3%-5% conversions.

Of course, your product or service could be a necessity, novelty, or other —ty that makes it convert much higher.

What kind of assumptions, you ask?

Well, for starters, you assume your headline is good. You assume your button placement is the best. You assume your offer resonates with your customers. You assume your copy is well written. You assume these and dozens of other things.

Those assumptions should be tested at every turn by data. You observe and react to the data. It doesn't matter what your gut says if the data doesn't back it up.

At times, the process can be tedious and discouraging. I want to let you know the tangible benefits you'll receive as a result of an optimized landing page. Look back at this list when you get tired of the optimization process and want to throw in the towel.

It'll always be worth it.

Benefits of Landing Pages

I'm only going to touch on a few of the many benefits of landing pages. There are so many, I could write a book solely on this.

I digress.

The versatility of landing pages is what makes them so powerful. You can change colors, fonts, images, copy, and anything else you want with just a few keystrokes and button clicks.

Try doing that with the design you paid your developer for. Or what about the marketing videos you're thinking about making. How hard will those be to change?

Anyway, let's move into the most powerful positives of landing pages.

Skyrocket Website Conversions

What if you had a three-page website? One page is your homepage. The other page is your about page. The last page is a landing page optimized for sales. You may convert at a few percentage points. More likely, you'll convert at below a percentage point.

What happens when you have dozens of landing pages in addition to the three pages I just mentioned?

You have one for giving away an e-book, you have another one for a nice tool, another one gives away a piece of software. Oh, I forgot the one you have for a free consultation. Together, the dozens of landing pages bring more than 10x your subscriber conversion rate.

Every subscriber you gain is another opportunity for a sale. With email marketing, you'll blow your normal conversion rate out of the water.

This isn't a book on email marketing, but the two go hand in hand. The increased conversions via landing pages, coupled with a strong email marketing campaign will do wonders for your bottom line.

Data gathering and usage behavior

It's the internet. We're all connected. Whether that's good for us as individuals is up for debate. There's no denying its good news for your business.

Imagine you're getting poor conversions on your product pages. You drill down into the data and realize most of your visitors are using Chrome and Safari browsers. You also notice you're getting much better conversion rates from visitors using Firefox and Internet Explorer.

You could ignore it, but you dive deeper and realize the difference is statistically significant (that means it's not a fluke).

You use an Android device and Mozilla Firefox when you access your pages. You've not experienced any issues when browsing.

You forget about it and start doing something else. While you're working, you can't shake the feeling that something's wrong. You can't ignore what you saw, so you borrow your friends iPhone and navigate to your landing page.

The images aren't lining up well, the text is off center, and the page looks like it was dug up from the nineties.

You're stunned.

You download Google Chrome and navigate to the page. The same thing happens. Elements aren't where they're supposed to be, your font colors are off, and it looks like a child put the page together.

You're mortified.

How many people saw this page and decided your business sucked? After all, what kind of company can't even put a page together correctly?

You figured out an important piece of information with just one data point. Imagine what you can do when you have multiple data points to compare.

Sure, Google analytics gives you information, but dedicated landing page software gives you the data you need without having to prepare tedious custom reports. I've been there; it's not fun or easy.

This is a more extreme example, but when you have accurate data to work with, you'll begin to understand gaps and see patterns you can exploit.

Better Data Backed Decisions

With better data come better decisions. I talked about the ability to gather data at the last point. Now, I want to talk about what you can do with that data. In business, you need to know your costs and the effectiveness of your distribution channels, right?

If a direct mail piece is pulling $500 in profit for every one-hundred spent, you'll ramp it up – right?

The same applies to the web. If your Facebook ad campaign is pulling in profits then you'll put more money behind it.

Of course.

With the vast amount of data you'll be able to collect, like where people came from, which ones became customers, which traffic source bounced, how long they stayed on the page, etc. you'll make better decisions.

How would you change your campaigns if you realized the thousand dollars you spent on Facebook was only bringing in half as much as the thousand you spend on Instagram?

I bet you'd cut your Facebook ad spend and refocus it on Instagram.

Your decisions cease to be made based on how you feel. They become decisions you're confident in. It's no longer "we do it like this because it's always been done like this" to "we do it like this because we've run the tests."

You make better decisions when you have better data. Hold your data inviolate.

Build Hype and Validate Products/Ideas

How do you think people feel about your product or service? Unless it's a matter of life or death, it'll get old.

When Facebook appeared on the scene, it didn't have one-tenth of the bells and whistles it does now. It was a place to catch up with friends and follow companies you like. Now, there are ads everywhere, you keep getting requests to play games, and it tracks your movements in the real world.

It's a bit creepy.

Even though we criticize the way Facebook has changed, it wouldn't be here today if it would've stayed the same.

No matter what you're doing or selling, you need to create variety in your business.

If you've had only a few products, landing pages are a way to introduce new products gradually while testing market feedback.

If your blog is playful and laid back, landing pages are an outlet to get down to serious business. It's your choice how you introduce variety. Landing pages just happen to be an amazing vehicle for it.

Cater to more User Segments

This follows on the heels of variety. You may have one or only a few products and not need anymore. Even if that's the case, your customers will use your product differently.

Take Pinterest for example.

The main website was built for a certain demographic of people. Those are well to do, educated, and married women. In 2017, men have become the largest growing segment of their user base.

Those are for the users — the buyers. They have another section of their website entirely for advertisers and business owners. These people are the ones who are paying the bills and need resources and tools to make the most out of Pinterest.

It's not limited to marketplace type businesses or social media. Think about a photographer. They take pictures at weddings, birthdays, bar mitzvahs, and everything in between. When someone lands on their website, they want information relating to their specific situation. They don't want the generic spiel.

You can apply the same principle to almost any industry. The financial services sector needs different faces for students, young workers, high net worth individuals, and businesses.

The construction industry builds retail spaces, homes, and multi-unit housing complexes. Do you think those people need the same information? No, they don't. They need content, images, and offers related to their specific situation.

Even if you don't have dozens of products, you have different user segments which have different needs. The more optimized landing pages you have, the more opportunities there are to connect with different market segments.

Improve Marketing Campaigns

One of my biggest pet peeves is clicking on a link for a specific item and being dumped on the homepage. Yes, the homepage may have some of the information I'm looking for, but I have to keep clicking to get the entire story.

Why?

Why would you make me do extra work? Every extra step I have to take is an added layer of resistance. Unless I'm a highly motivated buyer, I'm likely to bounce and never return.

The good news is that most websites are waking up and sending individuals to specific landing pages: not all, but most.

Landing pages improve marketing campaigns because you're able to drill down into the needs of a specific group of people. It can be a campaign which deals with your new vacuum cleaner, but there are different types of people who need it.

You have the single mom, you have the college student, and you have the elderly couple.

For each of these groups, you'll highlight different benefits to the potential customer. For the single mom, it could be how affordable and durable it is. For the elderly couple, you can touch on how quiet and easy to use it is. You can lead with low maintenance and its chic design when talking to college students (and how cheap it is).

Every marketing campaign and segment within that campaign should have a dedicated landing page. I know that's not always possible for various reasons. Chief of which is data and time, but it's something to strive for when optimizing your pages.

Put List Building on Steroids

This is the most popular use of your landing pages. It's almost as important as using them for sales pages.

Almost.

The sidebar on your website works, but many people experience blindness. Think about how you personally use websites. Do you give the sidebar more than a passing glance?

No?

Neither does the rest of the world. Most websites don't make it worth your time. They add ugly graphics, uglier opt-in forms, and the occasional greatest hits collection. < what does this mean in context?

On average, the sidebar conversion rate hovers between 0.5% and 1%. Those are good numbers. Most websites don't achieve that without rigorous testing.

Dedicated landing pages are a different beast. On average, conversion rates climb well into the teens. For every 100 people that visit a landing page created to get contact details, 15-20 of them will become email subscribers.

I'm sure you know as well as I do that email subscribers are the bread and butter of cost-effective marketing campaigns.

With an optimized landing page, those numbers can easily double or triple. It's not by accident. A landing page focuses the attention and gives your prospect two options.

Either they perform your desired action or they exit the page. There aren't a bunch of miscellaneous links for them to click on, no menu buttons, and only one call to action.

Improve Credibility

Last but not least, landing pages improve your credibility in the eyes of your visitors.

Let me explain.

Throughout your website, you have elements scattered about. Maybe you have featured logos on the about page and homepage.

You also have testimonials on different portions of your website. They work together to let the people visiting know you're credible. In addition to that, you have a great design and other things going for you.

With a landing page, you incorporate those elements into one page.

You have testimonials, featured logos, and a unique design all on one page. You use persuasive language and pull out the big guns to establish trust.

Instead of someone needing to navigate to the homepage, then the about page, then the testimonials page, and maybe a few blog posts, you do the work for them with a well-designed landing page. It's a shortcut to the credibility needed to make a sale.

In a nutshell, landing pages are an asset. The more you have, the greater your conversions across the board. In a 2016 study, it was discovered that conversions went up by 55% once a website had ten or more landing pages.

That means just one landing page won't cut it. Five landing pages won't cut it either. It's a constant process of creation and iteration. Throughout the rest of this book, you're going to be equipped with the insights and strategies to turn your landing pages into works of art.

*Want to read more? Check our book '**Content Marketing: Growth Strategies to Stay Ahead in the Changing World of Content Marketing and Maximize ROI**' on Amazon today!*

References

Bhatt, D. (2018, March). *A quick comparison of the five best big data frameworks.* Retrieved from https://opensourceforu.com/2018/03/a-quick-comparison-of-the-five-best-big-data-frameworks/

Brownie, J. (2019, September). Machine Learning Mastery. *A tour of the most popular machine learning algorithms.* Retrieved from https://machinelearningmastery.com/a-tour-of-machine-learning-algorithms/

Chartio. (ND). *Types of data analysis.* Retrieved from https://chartio.com/learn/data-analytics/types-of-data-analysis/

Donges, N (2018, March). Towards Data Science. *Data types in statistics.* Retrieved from https://towardsdatascience.com/data-types-in-statistics-347e152e8bee

Eneriz, A. (2018, November). Northeastern University. *11 Data science careers shaping our future.* Retrieved from https://www.northeastern.edu/graduate/blog/data-science-careers-shaping-our-future/

Expert System. (ND). *What is machine learning? A definition.* Retrieved https://www.expertsystem.com/machine-learning-definition/

Goh, E. (2018, December). Lead. *5 Steps to a data science project lifecycle.* Retrieved from https://www.thelead.io/data-science/5-steps-to-a-data-science-project-lifecycle

Han Lau, C. (2019, January). Towards Data Science. *5 Steps of a data science project lifecycle.* Retrieved from https://towardsdatascience.com/5-steps-of-a-data-science-project-lifecycle-26c50372b492

Harlalka, R. (2018, June). *Choosing the right machine learning algorithms.* Retrieved from https://hackernoon.com/choosing-the-right-machine-learning-algorithm-68126944ce1f

Helmenstine, A. M. (2019, August). Thought Co. *Bayes Theorem definition and examples.* Retrieved from https://www.thoughtco.com/bayes-theorem-4155845

Hopkins, J. (2019, July). Top Coder. *The data science life cycle.* Retrieved from https://www.topcoder.com/blog/the-data-science-life-cycle/

Jayathilaka, M. (2019, May). Towards Data Science. *How to make your data science presentation great and memorable.* Retrieved from https://towardsdatascience.com/how-to-make-your-data-science-presentation-great-and-memorable-8fdb07978a7e

Kobielus, J. (2018, March). *Big data analytics: The cloud-fueled shift now underway.* Retrieved from https://www.infoworld.com/article/3261145/big-data-analytics-the-cloud-fueled-shift-now-under-way.html

Koehrsen, W. (2018, September). *Introduction: Hyperparameter tuning using grid and random search.* Retrieved from https://www.kaggle.com/willkoehrsen/intro-to-model-tuning-grid-and-random-search

Lehr, S. (2019, August). *20 inspiring quotes about data.* Retrieved from https://www.ringlead.com/blog/20-inspirational-quotes-about-data/

NewTech Dojo (2018, August). *Components of data science.* Retrieved from https://www.newtechdojo.com/components-of-data-science/

Malik, M. (2018, April). Becoming Human. *Basics of Neural Network.* Retrieved from https://becominghuman.ai/basics-of-neural-network-bef2ba97d2cf

MathWorks (ND). *What is deep learning? 3 Things you need to know.* Retrieved from https://www.mathworks.com/discovery/deep-learning.html

Minitab. (2017, April). *Understanding qualitative, quantitative, attribute, discrete, and continuous data types.* Retrieved from https://blog.minitab.com/blog/understanding-statistics/understanding-qualitative-quantitative-attribute-discrete-and-continuous-data-types

Nautiyal, D. (ND). *The 5 best programming languages for artificial intelligence.* Retrieved from https://www.geeksforgeeks.org/top-5-best-programming-languages-for-artificial-intelligence-field/

Phong Gandecha, T. (2018m August). Towards Data Science. *The three cores of data science.* Retrieved from https://towardsdatascience.com/the-three-cores-of-data-science-d58af0d7361e

Ravanshad, A. (2018, April). *How to choose machine learning algorithms.* Retrieved from https://medium.com/@aravanshad/how-to-choose-machine-learning-algorithms-9a92a448e0df

Seif, G. (2018, March). Towards data science. *5 types of regression and their properties.* Retrieved from https://towardsdatascience.com/5-types-of-regression-and-their-properties-c5e1fa12d55e

Software testing help (ND). *11 most popular machine learning software tools in 2019.* Retrieved from https://www.google.com/amp/s/www.softwaretestinghelp.com/machine-learning-tools/amp/

Supply Chain Today. (2019, March). *Artificial intelligence and machine learning quotes from top minds.* Retrieved from http://www.supplychaintoday.com/artificial-intelligence-machine-learning-quotes-top-minds/

Udacity. (ND). *How to write a professional data analysis report.* Retrieved from https://career-resource-center.udacity.com/portfolio/data-science-reports

Zola, A. (2019, June). *41 Shareable data quotes that will change how you think about data.* Retrieved from https://www.springboard.com/blog/41-shareable-data-quotes/